CAMBRIDGE LIBRARY COLLECTION

Books of enduring scholarly value

Egyptology

The large-scale scientific investigation of Egyptian antiquities by Western scholars began as an unintended consequence of Napoleon's invasion of Egypt during which, in 1799, the Rosetta Stone was discovered. The military expedition was accompanied by French scholars, whose reports prompted a wave of enthusiasm that swept across Europe and North America resulting in the Egyptian Revival style in art and architecture. Increasing numbers of tourists visited Egypt, eager to see the marvels being revealed by archaeological excavation. Writers and booksellers responded to this growing interest with publications ranging from technical site reports to tourist guidebooks and from children's histories to theories identifying the pyramids as repositories of esoteric knowledge. This series reissues a wide selection of such books. They reveal the gradual change from the 'tomb-robbing' approach of early excavators to the highly organised and systematic approach of Flinders Petrie, the 'father of Egyptology', and include early accounts of the decipherment of the hieroglyphic script.

The Rock Tombs of Deir el Gebrâwi

While working as a Congregational minister in England, Norman de Garis Davies (1865–1941) developed an interest in Egyptology. In 1897 he joined Flinders Petrie's excavations at Dendera as a copyist of inscriptions and sculptures. He did further work for the Egypt Exploration Fund, producing many volumes of archaeological surveys, which won him the Leibniz medal of the Prussian Academy of Sciences. From 1907 he worked for New York's Metropolitan Museum of Art, together with his wife Nina. Highly illustrated, this two-volume 1902 publication covers the tombs of the important Old Kingdom necropolis at Deir el-Gabrawi, where many of the governors of the Upper Egyptian 12th nome were buried. Volume 1 covers the southern group of tombs, including that of the nomarch Aba. Davies reproduces the tomb art and hieroglyphic inscriptions, as well as providing archaeological plans. His *Rock Tombs of Sheikh Saïd* (1901) is also reissued in this series.

T0371353

The Rock Tombs
of Deir el Gebrâwi

Volume 1: Tomb of Aba and
Smaller Tombs of the Southern Group

Norman de Garis Davies

Cambridge
University Press

CAMBRIDGE
UNIVERSITY PRESS

University Printing House, Cambridge, CB2 8BS, United Kingdom

Cambridge University Press is part of the University of Cambridge.

It furthers the University's mission by disseminating knowledge in the pursuit of
education, learning and research at the highest international levels of excellence.

www.cambridge.org
Information on this title: www.cambridge.org/9781108080231

© in this compilation Cambridge University Press 2015

This edition first published 1902
This digitally printed version 2015

ISBN 978-1-108-08023-1 Paperback

This book reproduces the text of the original edition. The content and language reflect
the beliefs, practices and terminology of their time, and have not been updated.

Cambridge University Press wishes to make clear that the book, unless originally published
by Cambridge, is not being republished by, in association or collaboration with,
or with the endorsement or approval of, the original publisher or its successors in title.

The original edition of this book contains a number of colour plates,
which have been reproduced in black and white. Colour versions of these
images can be found online at www.cambridge.org/9781108080231

TOMB OF ABA.

DANCING GIRLS—W. WALL.
(*See Plates IX. and X.*)

ARCHAEOLOGICAL SURVEY OF EGYPT

EDITED BY F. LL. GRIFFITH

ELEVENTH MEMOIR

THE ROCK TOMBS

OF

DEIR EL GEBRÂWI

PART I.—TOMB OF ABA AND SMALLER TOMBS OF
THE SOUTHERN GROUP

BY

N. DE G. DAVIES

TWENTY-SIX PLATES AND FRONTISPIECE

SPECIAL PUBLICATION OF THE EGYPT EXPLORATION FUND

LONDON
SOLD AT
THE OFFICES OF THE EGYPT EXPLORATION FUND, 37, GREAT RUSSELL STREET, W.C.
AND 59, TEMPLE STREET, BOSTON, MASS., U.S.A.
AND BY KEGAN PAUL, TRENCH, TRÜBNER & CO., PATERNOSTER HOUSE, CHARING CROSS ROAD, W.C.
B. QUARITCH, 15, PICCADILLY, W.; ASHER & CO., 13, BEDFORD STREET, COVENT GARDEN, W.C.
AND HENRY FROWDE, AMEN CORNER, E.C.
—
1902

LONDON:
PRINTED BY GILBERT AND RIVINGTON, LTD.
ST. JOHN'S HOUSE, CLERKENWELL.

CONTENTS

——••——

LIST OF THE PLATES

WITH REFERENCES TO THE PAGES ON WHICH THEY ARE DESCRIBED.

——— •• ———

NOTE.—*The coloured plates are from paintings by Mr. Percy Buckman. Plates II. and IIA. are based on plans by Mr. John Newberry. The mural scenes have all been reproduced directly from tracings. Where possible, the colours have been indicated on the plates by initial letters, as follows :—*

b = blue ;   *y = yellow ;*   *w = white ;*   *bk = black ; and*

r = red ;   *or = orange ;*   *g = green ;*   *dr = drab (perhaps merely lack of colour).*

THE ROCK TOMBS

OF

DEIR EL GEBRÂWI

I.—INTRODUCTION

I. PREVIOUS WORK IN THE NECROPOLIS.

IT is rarely that under this heading the historian has to go back beyond the middle of the last century. He laments in vain that no one in the Middle Ages, whether of European or Arab birth, was impelled by curiosity or by a breadth of sympathy beyond his time to copy the ancient monuments of Egypt, which in those days must have been far more numerous and complete than now. Since the work of accurately reproducing these ancient master-pieces goes forward but tardily even in our days, this may seem an unreasonable reproach. Yet in the case of the tombs of Deir el Gebrâwi an acknowledgment is due to a time far earlier than the Christian centuries. The most interesting scenes in the tomb of Aba were copied in the days of Psammetichus I., who reigned in the VIIth century B.C.; a period standing about midway between the time of the VIth Dynasty and our own. In those days a prince of Thebes, Aba by name, was preparing for himself an elaborate tomb in the Theban necropolis; remembering that in the XIIth Nome there was a finely painted chapel of a namesake

of his, who had been an *erpa* prince like himself, he caused several scenes from it to be repro-duced on the walls of his own place of burial. He was moved to this, no doubt, partly because he was willing to claim this early nomarch as an ancestor, partly because he appreciated the un-usual merit and interest of the scenes, and largely also because it was the fashion of his age to imitate the art of the Ancient Kingdom. Though the copy is far from being, in any scientific or artistic sense, a replica of the original, the enterprise and appreciation shown by Aba are deserving of all praise; and, con-sidering the end in view, the closeness with which the original has been followed indicates no small respect for the ancient forms.[1]

The tombs seem to have been re-discovered by Mr. Harris of Alexandria in 1850, and to

---

[1] The tomb has been published by V. SCHEIL, *Tombeaux thébains*, pp. 624, *sqq.* Excerpts are also to be found in ROSELLINI, *Mon. Civ.*; CHAMPOLLION, *Mon.*, and *Not.* p. 553; LEPSIUS, *D.* iii. 271a, 272a, b; BRUGSCH, *Recueil*, ii. plate lxviii. The scenes in question have been recopied (Dec. 1901) for the present volume (plates xxiv. and xxv.), and their relation to the original are discussed in the appendix.

have been again visited by him in 1855.[1] Sir Gardner Wilkinson also paid a visit to the necropolis about this time, and his diaries contain copious extracts from the tomb of Zau. Brief information concerning them, gathered apparently from the tombs themselves, has for many years had a place in the standard guide books. Messrs. Petrie and Griffith also took notes in the northern necropolis in 1886.[2] In 1890 copies of the longer and more legible inscriptions in the tomb of Zau were made by Professor Sayce and published.[3] The expedition sent out by the Archaeological Survey under the charge of Mr. Percy Newberry in the winter of 1892 spent some time here, tracing the scenes in the tombs of Aba and Zau and taking notes of the more fragmentary records. Copies in colour of selected subjects were also made, and plans drawn. The promise of publication was, however, never fulfilled. Some years later Professor Sayce again visited the southern group, and published additional inscriptions from the two large tombs.[4] The copies bear everywhere the mark of notes gathered under conditions which quite precluded accuracy or completeness; and the reader who compares them with the present tracings will probably agree that, great as was the service done by these articles in calling attention to the historical importance of these monuments, the record cannot be taken very seriously. A considerable part of the commentary which M. Maspero appended to the earlier article also loses its force, as it is based on a conclusion which a fuller publication of the records directly contradicts.

The burial shafts in the tombs have been ransacked subsequently to 1893, with or without the sanction of the authorities, but assuredly by no competent person; for the rubbish had been piled up against the painted walls. It is to be hoped that the labour of these treasure-seekers was thrown away.

2. THE PRESENT UNDERTAKING.

As in 1899 the tombs still remained unpublished, it was proposed that this task should make part of my work for the Archaeological Survey in the winter of that year. Accordingly, after completing the work at Sheikh Saïd, I transferred my camp to this remote corner of the Nile Valley, reaching it on February 23rd, 1900. The little hamlet of Deir el Gebrâwi huddles round a church not long rebuilt on an ancient site, and has the distinction of being inhabited solely by Copts. The village being extremely unsavoury, I took up my abode in the uninscribed tomb No. 10, on the very summit of the cliff, and being here too far above the busy rural life of the plain to be disturbed even by the curious, was able to devote the ensuing seven weeks to the task before me. By continuous labour the whole of the paintings were traced within this time, and all the material gathered which was thought necessary for a complete publication of both groups. The discovery of additional designs beneath the dirt which in places covered the walls, made a revision of the work of my predecessors necessary, and as their tracings had suffered considerably during the long interval, it was found more satisfactory to recopy the whole. Fortunately I was able to avail myself of some excellent plans of the larger inscribed tombs which had been drawn by Mr. John Newberry in 1893, and to which I had only to add the result of such small clearances as I made. I left the neighbourhood on the 13th of April, 1900.

---

[1] Since the days of Wilkinson the tombs have been associated with Beni Mohammed el Kufur, but that village is several miles distant, nor is there any necessity to take it *en route.* The present title has therefore been adopted.

[2] I take the above information from Mr. Newberry's account, *Arch. Report,* 1892-3, p. 14.

[3] *Recueil de Travaux,* xiii. p. 65.

[4] *Ibid.,* xx. p. 169.

3. THE SITUATION OF THE NECROPOLIS.

The exact limits of the ancient nomes are little known, and the XIIth Nome certainly does not form an exception. But it may be said with some confidence that it must have included that broad expanse of fertile land, so rare on the eastern bank, which the receding hills here leave between them and the river, and of which Ebnub is the modern centre. It would extend, therefore, between Manfalût and Siût, but on the opposite bank. Slightly to the south of the former town, the eastern hills, which northward follow the river closely, fall back and take a course almost due east, the precipitous cliffs of the Gebel Qurneh marking the turning point. Eastward of this there is a slight bay in the line of hills, some three miles in breadth, from which a wady leads northward through the mountains to the plain of Tell el Amarna. The Arab village of El Atiyat, nestling under the towering wall of rock, marks one end of the horn; the tiny Coptic village of Deir el Gebrâwi, standing on the edge of the cultivation, opposite the steep, but not equally precipitous, heights of the Gebel Marag, forms the other. Midway between the two, where the mountains have less elevation, lies half the necropolis of Deir el Gebrâwi, the NORTHERN GROUP of tombs. Taking advantage of the fact that at this point the mountain slope was broken by a terrace, from which the rest of the cliff rose almost perpendicularly, the ancient inhabitants chose this site as a place of burial, and the tombs hewn in the wall of white stone are visible, like nests in the rock, far over the green plain. After some time, and probably with the incoming of a new reigning house, the necropolis was shifted to a point slightly to the east of Deir el Gebrâwi. Here again, almost at the summit of the lofty cliffs, there is a level surface backed by a low wall of rock. The tombs here, fifty-two in number, form the

SOUTHERN GROUP.[1] Of these, the tombs of Aba and Zau are large and fully decorated, and seven others retain inscriptions.[2] Of 104 tombs in the northern group only seven or eight show even a trace of inscription.

The tomb of Aba, together with all smaller tombs of the southern group, forms the subject of the present memoir. The painted chamber of Zau and the tombs of the northern group must be reserved for another volume.

4. THE TOMBS OF THE SOUTHERN GROUP.

(Plate i.)

As has just been remarked, the site of these tombs is on a terrace close under the summit of the mountain range, which here, opposite the hamlet of Deir el Gebrâwi, towers very steeply above the cultivation and at a comparatively short distance from it. Unless the inaccessibility of the site, or the magnificent view over the rich country southwards to Siut which it commands, attracted the princes of the nome to this spot, there seems little else to recommend it. The stone is of poor quality, hard boulders again and again disfiguring the work alike of quarryman and artist. The extent of any wall of rock too was very small, so that much material had to be cut away before the almost upright façade which was desired could be gained. But it seems almost a point of honour in the East that a change of rulers should be marked by a change of home, and it is not surprising that in Egypt this should be extended to the resting-place of the dead also. There was room here for the few princely tombs, and lesser men had to make the best of the site,

---

[1] The groups might with almost equal correctness be called western and eastern, but the designation adopted best suits Egypt.

[2] The assertion in Baedeker's *Egypt,* that there are twelve inscribed tombs, appears to be without warrant.

often excavating their small chambers in mere shelves of rock. The tombs lie along the low cliff in which Aba and Zau had hewn their spacious chambers, and then range themselves round a natural amphitheatre to the west, a gathering ground for the waters of occasional deluges, which have cut a deep channel down the cliff from this point. Besides the tombs shown on plate i., there are a few small uninscribed chambers low down the hillside, near the watercourse; and also a few caves, some of them natural, further westward, on the slope of the hills, near a ruined brick chapel.

As will be seen, these places of burial are generally small and rough, with but little exterior show. The interment was usually in a tiny chamber at the bottom of a shallow pit or shaft, less important members of the family or dependents being content with a little gallery hewn in the side of the tomb-chamber, or outside it altogether. Very few indeed could afford more than this, or thought of any other memorial than a tiny plastered and painted tablet containing a list of offerings, the banqueting scene, and a brief prayer.

A rock site does not invite elaborate architecture, nor permit it without large expenditure of labour; and as in the working of living stone the result may at any time be disfigured by the occurrence of natural faults, it is no wonder that the exteriors of the tombs, though still striving to imitate the façade of a brick-and-timber built house, are very simple, and often rough. In this respect, however, they compare unfavourably with the contemporary tombs at Sheikh Saïd. The façades of even the largest tombs here are much inferior to similar tombs on that site, and show no trace of sculpture on the exterior; they have departed much further from the typical work of the Ancient Kingdom in the sculptured figures of the entrance way, and the rock-cut statues which are so marked a feature of the Sheikh Saïd tombs are altogether absent. It was a transition period between decoration by sculpture and decoration by fresco painting. At Sheikh Saïd the latter was timidly employed (Tomb of Uau), and the use of bas-relief was not yet abandoned. In the southern tombs of Deir el Gebrâwi that step has been taken. Sculpture has disappeared, except for some rough incised figures in the doorways, but fresco painting has become the medium for elaborate schemes of decoration.

5. LIST OF TOMBS OF THE SOUTHERN GROUP.

The façades of the tombs are of three types, and where not stated to be otherwise, are formed with a slight batter.

Type A. The rock face is here merely smoothed to a plane surface for a foot or so on either side the entrance and to a smaller distance above it.

Type B. A projecting lintel band extends across the jambs immediately above the entrance.

Type C. The jambs are double, the inner ones being recessed. The lintel extends over both.

TYPE.

1. A. Small and low. A rough niche in the back wall. Floor not visible. Hewn in the sloping ground.
2. Tomb of HETEPNEB. See p. 24.
3. B. Hewn in the cliff. Very rough. Breach into Tomb 4.
4. Front worn away. Rough, low, and shapeless.
5. Back part of a gallery, or "mummy slide."
6. A. The excavation of the interior is scarcely begun.
7. B. (Plans on Plates ii. and ii.a.) The cliff is cut far back to give a lofty façade. The tomb was made subsequently to the tomb of Aba, the little chamber of the latter being

TYPE.

carefully avoided. It consists of a large square room, the walls of which have been carefully hewn, yet show no sign of inscription. Though the floor is not visible, the chamber is more than 11 feet in height; but as the roomy gallery which runs out of the N. wall is thus left high in air, and a rough ledge of rock runs all along the E. wall about 7 feet from the ceiling, the floor must originally have been higher. There is a deep rebate all round the doorway within.

8. B.   Tomb of ABA (see Pl. ii. *et seqq.*).

9.   (Plans on Plates ii. and ii.*a.*) The entrance shows no sign of a façade. The chamber is extremely rough within, and the partition wall on the E. has been broken through. Low down in the W. corner of the back wall there is a passage leading down to an inner room, 45 inches high, in the floor of which is a breach into the vault of the tomb of Aba.

10. B.   (Plan on Plate xxii.) Square door-lintel. A tomb carefully hewn without and within, but bearing no trace of inscription. There is a rebate round the door inside, as also round the shrine recess in the N. wall. The floor is not visible, but a pit seems to occupy the whole recess, from which a passage more than 18 feet in length leads to the burial chamber, as in the tomb of Aba. On the back wall of the shrine are Coptic crosses and daubs in red paint. The façade has a batter of 1 in 6. On the E. side of the approach is a tiny chamber at ground level, which

TYPE.

may have been a separate place of burial.

11.   (For plan see Plate i. and Vol. ii., Plate ii.) Nearly the whole of the front has fallen. The chamber is low and shapeless and the floor extremely irregular. Its excavation has caused the ruin of the S.E. corner of the tomb of Zau. Outside on the E. of the approach there is a niche which probably was made to hold some commemorative tablet.

12. A.   Tomb of ZAU. (For plans see Plate i. and Vol. ii., Plate ii.)

13. C.   A diminutive tomb, yet divided into two by a pilaster and false architrave. The east wall is extremely rough and full of boulders. There are three or four shafts, of which only the northernmost is at present empty. This is 9 feet 6 in. deep and expands below to the N.E., so as to form a little chamber at the bottom.

14. B.   (Plan on Plate xxi.) Tomb of UHA (?) See p. 24.

15.   (Plan on Plate xxi.) Its front is entirely broken away. It may have been merely a gallery, the low chamber to the W. being a separate burial place; or the two may have formed one tomb.

16. B.   (Plan on Plate xxi.) Tomb of TEKHYT. See p. 25.

17.   A niche 20 inches high. Lower down the slope.

18. B.   Only the façade has been completed; the interior is hardly begun.

19,20,21. (Plans on Plate xxii.) Small, low chambers. Their fronts and W. walls are broken down, and the floors covered with rubbish.

22. B. Square door-lintel. (Plans on Plate xxii.) The lower part of the walls of this tomb are broken away on both E. and W. It was originally rectangular in shape, but very irregularly hewn at the back, where a pit, now blocked with stones, appears to give entrance to a burial chamber towards the north. The entrance is set much further back in the cliff than its neighbours.

23. (Plan on Plate xxii.) A pit-tomb, entered from above and having a chamber to the north a few feet from the mouth, so that it is on the level of those around it. It is evidently earlier than these, for they have all avoided it; yet so narrowly that the thin partition walls are now broken through on all sides.

24. (Plan on Plate xxii.) The front is broken down. The low chamber was provided with two short galleries running from the N. wall, but the sides are now broken through in several places. There is a rebate round the eastern recess.

25. B. (Plan on Plate xxii.) Extremely irregular in shape, with very rough W. and N. walls and uneven floor. There are two or three shafts (now full), and a curving gallery runs from the N.E. corner. On the W. wall is a small plaster tablet, but nothing can be deciphered. The entrance has a rebate round it within.

26. A. (Square lintel in doorway.) Floor not visible. Tiny chamber with recess at the back. This and Tomb 27 are at a lower level.

27. Front gone. Roughly hewn. Floor not visible.

28. Tomb of SENBSEN. See p. 25.

29. Rough chamber excavated in shelving rock. Façade broken away.

30. A. A well-shaped tomb hewn in the overhanging cliff. Rough walls. Floor not visible.

31. Half the front destroyed. Very rough at back. Floor not visible.

32. (Plan on Plate xxii.). High in the cliff and reached by a sloping ascent. Rough outside and little more than a cave within. The W. wall has been mud-plastered. The shaft opens 5 feet from the mouth into a largish chamber, which is on the level of Tomb 33, and now accessible from it.

33. A. Square door lintel. (Plan on Plate xxii.) Tomb of MERUT. See p. 25.

34. B. Immediately over the doorway of Tomb 33, and on a level with Tomb 32. A recess 3 feet high, 2 feet broad and 4 feet deep. Evidently earlier than the tomb below, the construction of which has removed its means of access.

35. (Plan on Plate xxii.) A large rectangular tomb, 6 feet high. The façade is nearly destroyed. There are at least two burial shafts. An entrance to Tomb 37 has been cut in the W. wall. On the E. wall is a plaster tablet, but the surface is gone. To the left of the entrance outside is a small gallery, which must be earlier, as it has been avoided.

36. (Plan on Plate xxii.) A shallow pit-tomb with chamber to the N., earlier than Tomb 37, the S. wall of which is interfered with by

TYPE.

the chamber below (now nearly full).

37.　(Plan on Plate xxii.) Façade worn away. There is a shrine recess in the back wall with rebate all round. In the S.E. corner is a shaft which opens into a burial chamber on the N. side 4 feet from the mouth. The W. wall is irregular.

38. A.　Rough chamber excavated in a low slope. Floor not visible.

39.　Similar chamber. N. and E. walls very rough.

40.　Pit-tomb. Unfinished?

41. A.　(Plan on Plate xxi.) Tomb of NEFER-TEP-WA. See p. 26.

42. A.　(Plan on Plate xxi.) Tomb of NEFER-NEF-KHETU. See p. 26.

43, 44.　Two small and rough tombs in a dip of the hill, excavated in a rock surface with scarcely any slope, and so broken and buried that nothing more can be said of them.

45.　Pit-tomb, the chamber of which is reached 9 feet from the surface.

TYPE.

46. A.　(Plan on Plate xxi.) Far back on the summit of the hill. Now little more than a cave. Floor not visible. A modern wall of piled stones forms a little court in front.

47.　A small tomb nearly buried under stones.

48. A.　The back wall is now very rough. On the S. a chamber opens 7 feet below the ceiling, probably entered from a shallow pit; but the tomb is too deep in rubbish to ascertain this.

49.　Rough façade. A rude niche in the back wall. Floor not visible.

50. C.　(Plan on Plate xxi.) Small, but well-formed chamber. The well is empty for 11 feet.

51. C.　(Plan on Plate xxi.) Perhaps unfinished, the small excavation being but rough. The façade is rude and unsymmetrical.

52. A.　(Upright façade.) A well-hewn chamber, except that the back wall is rough, perhaps through decay. The floor is not visible.

II.—DESCRIPTION OF THE TOMBS

TOMB 8.

Belonging to 〈 〉 ABA.

(Plates I.—XX.)

Titles (commencing with those on Plates III. and XVIII. in order) :—

1. Hereditary Prince.
2. (Chief) Lector.
3. *Sem*-priest.
4. Master of every kind of Tunic.[1]
5. Great Chief of the Nome of This.
6. Superintendent of the South.
7. Superintendent of the two Granaries.
8. Superintendent of the two Fowling Pools.
9. Superintendent of the two Treasuries.
10. *Ha*-prince.[2]
11. He of the Great Residence.
12.* Favoured of the Hand.
13.* Director of the two Thrones.

14.† Director of . . . [3]
15.† He who is in the Chamber.
16. He who belongs to Nekhen.
17. Great Chief of Nekheb.
18.* Chief of the Pillared Hall.[4]
19.* Gate of Khonsu (?) [5]
20.* *Khu-á* (?).[6]
21.* Ruler of . . . [7]
22. Scribe of the Roll of the God (Temple Accountant ?).
23.* Director of every Divine Office.
24. Staff of Hapi (Apis Bull).
25. . . . . [8]

---

[1] Court Chamberlain and administrator of sumptuary laws?

[2] Usually placed second only to the title *erpa*. It is probably given the front place in the second row for prominence.

* Titles not held by Zau-Shmaa, but by his son Zau.

[3] Cf. Mariette, *Catalogue d'Abydos*, 524.

[4] But cf. Daressy, *Le Mastaba de Mera*, p. 541.

[5] Ib. p. 550, 564 ⟨ ⟩. This and the previous title are often associated, but are separable. So Vol. ii., Plate xiii.

[6] Cf. ⟨ ⟩, Mariette, *Cat. d'Abydos*, 525.

[7] Cf. *Le Mastaba de Mera*, p. 523; *Beni Hasan*, i., Plate xvii. Titles 20 and 21 are perhaps connected. For the sacred emblem see priest's insignia, Mariette, *Les Mastabas*, p. 465.

[8] Cf. *Le Mastaba de Mera*, pp. 550, 554, 569.

† Titles not held by either Zau, but peculiar to Aba.

26.* He who has power over Gods(?).

27.* Director of the depôts of the Crown of Lower Egypt.[1]

28. Superintendent of the distribution of divine offerings from the two Houses.[2]

29. Second Priest of the Men-ankh Pyramid of Neferkara.

30. Governor of the Residence.[3]

31. Royal Chancellor.

32. Sole Companion.

33. Great Chief of the *Du-ef* Nome.

34.† (?)

35.† *Ad mer.* Plate vi.

36.† Guiding (?) Star of Horus, Lord of Heaven.[4] Plate vi.

37.† Great in his Office, mighty in his Dignity.[5] Plate vi.

---

[1] *Le Mastaba de Mera*, pp. 523, 537, 550, 554, etc., where and other variants occur.

[2] simply on Plate xviii. Note the reading for the usual .

[3] The epithet "true" is here sometimes applied to titles 30, 31, 32, but perhaps could equally well have been added to any other.

[4] For the association of 35, 36, cf. *Le Mastaba de Mera*, pp. 537, 554, 565, 569. It will have been noticed that there is considerable coincidence in regard to rare titles between this tomb and that of Mera at Saqqareh. Perhaps Abydos was the native place of Mera and the scene of his earlier official career.

[5] Strangely enough, the animal is not here a goat but plainly an ass. The example supports von Calice's suggestion that the symbolism lies in the collar round the neck, not in the animal.

38. He who is over Secrets. Plate xix.

39. (?) Chief Priest of the Men-ankh Pyramid of Neferkara. Plate vii.

40. First after the King. Plate vii.

Names and Titles of his family :—

Wife.—Rahenem, whose good name is Henema. Plates xii., xviii.
"Sole Ornament of the King."
"Lady of the King."
"Acquaintance of the King."
"Priestess of Hathor, deserving before her mistress."

Daughters.—(1) Tekhyt. Plates iii., xvii.
"Lady of the King."
"Ornament of the King."
(2) Mertab. Plate xvii.
"Lady of the King."
(3) Henut. Plates v., xvii.
"Lady of the King."
"Sole Ornament of the King."
(4) Serezyt. Plate xvii.
"Sole Ornament of the King."

Sons.—(1) Zau, whose good name is Shmaa.
"Eldest." Plates v., xv.
"Royal Chancellor."
"Governor of the Residence."
"Sole Companion."
"Great Chief of the *Du-ef* Nome."
"Lector."
(2) Khua. Plates iii., xv.
"Governor of the Residence."
"Sole Companion."
"Lector."
(3) Aba. "Eldest." Plate iii.
"Governor of the Residence."
"Sole Companion."
"Lector."

(4) Zau.   Plates xv., xviii.
   "(Official) of the Great House,
      Semsu hayt."
(5) Aba.   Plate xvi.
   "Sole Companion."
(6) Zau.   Plates iii., xvi.
   "Sole Companion."
(7) Ada.   Plates iii., xvi.
   "Sole Companion."

Brother.—Zau.   Plates iii., xi.
   "(Official) of the Great House,
      Semsu hayt."

As will be seen from Plate ii.*a*, the façade of the Tomb of Aba is of the simplest type. The rock slope has been cut back, so as to give an elevation with slight batter. Then, for a considerable space in the centre, the rock has been a little more deeply recessed, leaving a broad jamb on either side of the doorway and a clear space above it below the projecting band of stone, which represents the lintel of the traditional façade. The recessed face is almost perpendicular. The exterior is not adorned by sculpture, save that low down on the right-hand jamb a "chief scribe" (?) of the Middle Kingdom, named Amenemhat, has recorded his name above a little niche, in which an inscribed tablet, or other memorial, may have been placed (Plate xxiii.).

There is a deep rebate all round the doorway within. Both sides of the entrance (A and B, Plate ii.) are sculptured with figures of Aba and his wife, but the work, besides being of very rough execution, is now greatly damaged. The method adopted is that of low relief on a sunk surface (relief *en creux*), which is unusual at this period. The outline of the figures also is scarcely of the familiar type of the Old Kingdom, and the same may be said of the attitude of the figure of Zau in the doorway of the neighbouring tomb. But this may only indicate that the feeling for that type of sculp-

ture had already passed, or was passing away. On the right (A) a male figure with protruding stomach stands facing outwards, wearing the simple tunic, short wig and collar. A female figure, of equal height, in short wig and the customary dress, stands behind him and embraces him with her left arm. A Coptic cross and a hieratic graffito occupy the space above.[1] On the left (B) is a somewhat similar group. The female figure, which is here shown by a column of hieroglyphs above to be that of "his beloved wife, the Sole Royal Ornament, the deserving Henema" (?), is of much smaller size. She carries a stem of papyrus, or a sceptre of that form (see Vol. ii., Plates vi. and x.). Of the lines of hieroglyphs over the head of the male figure parts of two remain (Pl. xxiii.), (1) *yw r sbt ḥr-f m ntr*.[2] (2) " . . . Rahenem (?) whom he loves . . . he who does what is commanded, Aba " (?). A "servant of the Ka," named Asa (Assa?), seems to have faced the figure of Aba.

The tomb consists of a large oblong chamber, having a deep recess in the back wall, which served as a shrine or special place of worship; as may be judged from the representations and false doors on each of its walls. Provision is made for burial in at least three places in the tomb; the rubbish which encumbers parts of the floor may possibly conceal others. The main vault is reached by a long gallery which extends northwards[3] from the back of the shrine, beginning as a depression in the floor. Descending gently, it terminates twenty-eight feet from the mouth in a level passage; and here a pit for burial, representing a sunk

---

[1] As the ink of these hieratic graffiti is invariably almost obliterated by time, they can only be satisfactorily read or copied by an expert in this script. I shall, therefore, note their occurrence in the hope that before long they will be made the object of separate study.

[2] Cf. *Griffith, Siut;* Tomb iv., l. 78; Tomb iii., l. 60.

[3] For convenience of description, throughout the volume the tomb is supposed to face directly south.

sarcophagus, is found in a recess on the left side.[1] A second vault is entered from a shallow pit in the north-west corner of the main chamber, from which a passage runs westward for a short distance. The vault is practically only a continuation of this low passage, at right angles to its former direction. It is almost empty. A representation and list of offerings in honour of Aba's wife Henema (Plate ix.), close to the mouth of the pit, indicates that this was her place of burial. A similar provision for burial is made on the opposite side of the chamber, but the entrance is now blocked with rubbish. Owing to the proximity of the next tomb, the vault to which the pit gives access cannot be larger than the rough little chamber which has been added on this side as an annexe to the large room. A short gallery at floor level in the centre of the western part of the north wall may also have received a coffin.

Though the tomb of Aba in its present state resembles that of Zau, when complete it must have been substantially different: an inch or so of two square pillars still depends from the roof, and the line of a false architrave connects them with each other and with a corresponding pilaster on the E. wall, while a line on the floor roughly corresponds to these traces above; for from this point backwards the floor of the chamber is several inches higher, being reached by an ascending slope in the middle of the room. Thus the two pillars, as seen from the entrance, would have appeared to be connected by an architrave above and a dwarf wall below.[2] Although there is no trace of a corresponding pilaster on the W. side, it was evidently the original plan that two pillars should support the roof, and divide the room into two halves

[1] This sloping gallery may be a reminiscence from brick mastabas such as those of Adu I. and other princes at Dendereh.

[2] The rubbish in the western half of the chamber did not allow a section of the floor to be taken on this side.

longitudinally. The ceiling is very irregularly hewn, dropping suddenly in the S.W. corner, and growing gradually higher towards the N.E. The large boulders occurring in the rock, which in several places interfere with the construction and decoration of the tomb, may partly account for this.

The tomb is adorned with paintings on the upper part of all its walls with the exception of the N. half of the E. wall, where a large boulder and the doorway of the small chamber left scarcely any space available. The paintings are executed on a surface of fine plaster, so excellently united with the rock surface that there are few places where it has fallen away. The aspect of the paintings is very different from those in the tomb of Zau and much less pleasing, the background being of that dark indigo hue which renders other colours almost invisible at any distance. Close and repeated scrutiny is necessary in order to secure all the detail. The paintings do not appear to have received any wilful damage in modern times; but the bats have destroyed the upper part of the scenes in the west half of the N. wall, and the E. wall with the east end of the S. wall have also greatly suffered from decay. A wide breach made in the partition wall between this tomb and No. 9 on the west, has destroyed a great part of the scenes at that point.

No order can be detected in the assignment of the various scenes to their respective walls, except that the walls of the shrine have been reserved for the subjects which were most closely concerned with the cult of the dead, and therefore most indispensable. For the main chamber were reserved the scenes which were less directly connected with the maintenance of the offerings. Here are depicted the cultivation of the soil, the care of domestic animals and birds, the capture of game, fish, and fowl, the administration of the estate and the supervision of the craftsmen whose handiwork was serviceable to the dead as well as to the living;

finally, the funeral ceremonies, and the record of rank and wealth.

South Wall. East Half. (Plates iii. and iv.).

The scene is thus characterized :—

" Seeing the work of the field, the capture of fish, the spearing. . . ."

Aba, in short sporting tunic, and with a holiday fillet bound round his head, stands on the alert in a large papyrus canoe, which has been urged through the thick trailing water-weeds (red, with green leaves, and a blue disc at the point of junction). It was not within the power of the artist to depict the rapid sequence of movement from the light poising of the spear on the finger-tips to the moment when, driven by the forefinger to its aim, it is raised in triumph with its double booty secure upon the prongs. Yet he has so depicted the final attitude as to suggest the action which preceded. As the fish were speared when in the water beneath, he simply encloses them in a mass of rippled blue. Aba's " eldest and beloved son " Zau is depicted in front of his father, in precisely the same dress and attitude; nor is his good fortune or skill in sport any less. Room is found in the crowded boat also for Aba's wife Henema and his daughter Tekhyt. Their hair is bound with fillets, and the daughter is enjoying the fragrance of a lotus-flower.

The four younger sons and the brother of Aba are seen behind, each holding a bird as if for presentation. It is evident that the family of Aba is introduced, not because they used to accompany him in this way on his sporting excursions, nor only in order to give importance to his figure here. Though the dead man had done with sport, he still had an interest in the spoils of living sportsmen. Aba, who probably caused the paintings to be executed while life still permitted him such pursuits, followed a natural instinct in making himself the central figure of the scene ; but the group of male relations holding out offerings of game not directly connected with the sport depicted, suggests that the picture is really a reminder to his posterity of the offerings of fish and wildfowl due to the dead. If such pictures disposed the son and the remoter members of the family to feel the towering figure of the dead asserting its undiminished claims even in their sport, their place in tomb decoration needs no other explanation.

These members of the family are ranked in order of importance. Khua, the second son, is immediately behind his father, and near him on the further side (above) is Aba, who is also styled " eldest." Behind them again is a brother of Aba, Zau. By his side (above) is still another Zau, and a son Ada follows.[1]

Fishing in the marshes was, however, more than a pastime of nobles. There is therefore added here, as generally, the scene in which the great drag-net, loaded below by stones tied to the edge and supported above by floats of some kind (yellow), is drawn to land filled with the fish and water-plants which have become entangled in it. Two companies of four men each, stationed on the bank at some distance from each other, have caused the net to sweep the pool by drawing its ends towards the shore

---

[1] Plates xv., xvi. add yet a third son Zau to the list, who bears the peculiar title given to the brother. We may suspect, therefore, that this is a mistake (though repeated on Plate xviii). To avoid still having two sons named Zau and two named Aba in the family, we might take it that the Zau, Aba, and Adu behind the brother are his sons, not Aba's. But the difficulty is a modern creation; to the Egyptian apparently there was none, though cases so flagrant as this do not often occur. In a tomb at Aswan three sons named Heqab are distinguished as " Heqab " simply, " the middle Heqab," and " the little Heqab " (Budge, P.S.B.A., 1887, page 33). As Dr. Walker points out to me, boys at our public schools are not assigned any greater measure of identity. The " good name " may have been added at the putting on of the girdle as an acknowledgment of personality.

and towards one another. The circuit is now completed, and while three at each end drag the net on shore, one is "closing the mouth of the net . . .", that none of the fish may escape. As, strictly speaking, the net is in the pool still, the water in it is indicated by broad horizontal bands of a darker blue. Those who haul are provided with a woven shoulder strap, which they attach to the cable, and so ensure a much more effective hold upon it.[1] To the left of these are three men poling a canoe along, and in the register below fishing with the hand-net is shown. The artist has placed within this net specimens of six of the eight species of fish which can be distinguished in the water here. (For details see Plate xxi.) The canoe in which the fisherman and his comrade stand is of a less usual shape, only the stern being elevated.

Along the whole length of the scene is a shallow strip of water, marked originally by vertical zig-zag lines of darker blue. It is occupied by fish, crocodiles, and hippopotamus, each of which is given the full size allowed by the depth of the water, regardless of the immense natural disproportions. The fish are admirably drawn, and seem to have been skilfully painted also, though there was probably only a rough approximation to nature in this respect. An artistic touch is also added by the introduction of lotus flowers and buds into the vacant spaces. In its original brightness of colour this strip of water must have supplied a charming border to the rest of the design.

The upper part of the wall here is occupied by a seated figure of Aba, before whom eight men stand in respectful attitudes, while fresh and cured fish are presented to him. The artist could not refrain from introducing also the

favourite subject of the quarrel between crews of passing boats, although it intrudes very awkwardly between two men who are engaged in cutting open the fish on a board, cleaning them and spreading them in the sun to dry. (See Plate xx. for the coloured reproduction.) "Cutting open fish" is the legend attached to this action; that over the men who are sparring is "Strike, strike . . . boatmen." A man, bearing on his shoulders a yoke from which fish hang, faces Aba. The superscription is not decipherable, but the general intention is indicated above by the words "for the *Ka* of the *Ha*-prince Aba." Only so much of the signs attached to the figures in the top register remains as enables a "superintendent of writing" to be identified. The inscription above describes them as "his brethren (?) of the place of his heart, who do his pleasure, (deserving) before their masters."

SOUTH WALL, WEST HALF (Plates v. and vi.).

This is devoted to the corresponding subject of fowling in the marshes. The boat, the water weeds, the inhabitants of the pool, are almost exactly similar. The figure of Aba differs only in the action of the arms, his right hand being held aloft in the act of hurling the throw-stick into the dense mass of birds which rise out of the thicket of papyrus as the boat is pushed towards it, filling the air with petals, struck by their wings from the flowering plants. In his left hand Aba holds two birds which he has secured.[2] Two other figures face him, his son Khua and his brother Zau (?), each holding birds towards him. Henut is here the daughter who accompanies her mother. The birds have to reckon not only with the human invaders of their quiet breeding places, but also with the

---

[1] See *Sheikh Saïd*, plate xii.; *El Bersheh*, i., plate xxii. In another case the means of attaching the shoulder strap to the rope is shown. European fishermen still use a similar contrivance.

[2] To be restored from the corresponding figure of his son Zau who stands on the prow.

little genet-cats which make their way up the slender reeds, and pillage the eggs and young. The introduction of this incident was no doubt due to the feeling for nature in some past master of the craft, and the approval of succeeding generations of copyists is shown by its almost invariable inclusion in the scene. The descriptive column runs, "The prince . . . Aba surveying the labour of the fields, traversing the backwaters, bringing down the nestlings (?) and birds with the throwstick." [1]

Behind the figure of Aba are represented (1) men bringing the produce of the marsh lands, birds and cattle; (2) the occupants of a canoe practising with the quarter-staff (?); (3) bearers of birds and flowers being ferried across the pool by comrades; (4) a man carrying a calf upon his back, and another with his staff of office, being transported in fishing punts, one of which is poled along, the other paddled. A phrase common in such ferrying scenes is written above—

$$ \text{𓀀𓎡𓅃𓏏𓊍𓊌𓏭𓏭} $$

" It is a herdsman whose face is alive with regard to the pool " (i.e. who is on the alert for crocodiles, etc.). The rest of the wall is occupied by a second portion of the scene, which is turned towards a sitting figure of Aba. His head is bound with a fillet, and he wears the close-fitting tunic.

The netting of birds, which ordinarily accompanies the scene just described, is relegated to the top of the wall, and seems to have been unintelligently copied from a scene in which the net was to the left hand; for the man who gives the signal by means of a cloth is behind instead of in front of his comrades, and is receiving no attention. The next scene shows

three groups engaged in gathering fruit from trees. From the context it might be supposed that these were a wild growth, but in a similar scene in the tomb of Asa the tree evidently bears figs or pomegranates, and stands among trellised vines (Vol. ii., Plate xvii.). The three registers below show great bundles of papyrus stems being carried away, and men, loaded with their booty of wildfowl, lotus flowers and sacks (of green fodder?), being ferried over the water. During the passage an osier fish-trap which had been laid previously in the water is raised to the surface. " Removing the fish-trap."[2] Over the second boat is " Paddling towards (?) the bull." The animal referred to is seen below, but must be taken in connection with the boat in Plate v. The cattle are thus seen not to be under the water, as at first appears, but wading through it; the calf of the herd, as usual, is supported by its forelegs by the man in the stern of the boat. The inscription, which no doubt referred to the aquatic enemy who is lying in force below, is obliterated. On the extreme right two men are fishing from a punt. One is evidently angling, the other, who is throwing his weight on a line, may be assisting his comrades alongside to raise the fish-trap, for success with the hook does not yet seem assured to him.

WEST WALL (Plates viii., ix., and x).

Three subjects are shown on this wall, so far as we can judge from that portion of it which the great breach has spared. On the right (Plate viii.) Aba sits to attend to the management of his property, and receive reports. The sitting is apparently held in the open court of the residence, for the fullers of cloth are busy with their occupation, and musicians are also present

---

[1] For the words used cf. L.D. ii. 61. See also LEVI *Vocabulario*, Suppl. ii., p. 52, for references for the word *Ama*.

[2] Read 𓂽𓏭𓊌 followed by the picture sign. So in the tombs of Thy and Kagemna at Saqqareh.

to relieve the tedium of business. A second scene is contained in the two upper registers of the left half of the wall. Aba is being carried in state in a roofed litter borne on staves by attendants. He carries the scourge as an emblem of authority, and is preceded and followed by two servants carrying flabella. (See Plate x. and Vol. ii., Plate viii.) These instruments appear to consist of a rectangular frame carried at the head of a long pole and having a white fringe attached to one side. As the worn inscription over the bearers ends with the words "They say," their customary chant was probably written under the litter, as in the corresponding scene in the tomb of Zau (Vol. ii., Plate viii.). In front of the palanquin a band of male and female dancers march with dance and song, headed by "the steward, superintendent of the toilette bag (?), superintendent of . . . . who is in the heart of his master . . . . ."[1] Six or more male singers follow, clapping their hands, while behind or beside them dancing girls perform in couples, headed by a leader who executes a *pas seul*. These performers are dressed in an apron resembling that worn by the half-nude fishermen, and have the professional headgear (a red ball or disc attached to the long tress), which seems to be an exaggerated imitation of the mode adopted for little girls.[2] This scene is clearly severed from that on the right by means of a border, and it seems equally separate in subject from the three registers below, which exhibit the funeral procession by land and water. The honours paid to the prince when carried on his tours of inspection, and the last honours paid to his body as he was borne to his tomb would seem very closely allied in the Egyptian mind. The head of the procession is seen on Plate viii., but

the accompanying inscription cannot be made out. The end of the scene shows the dragging of the bier, which consists of a wooden coffer set under a canopy and mounted on a sledge. It is drawn by embalmers, lectors, and others,[3] and during the passage incense is burnt before it. Above is " . . . . . in every place of his, he who is deserving before the great God, Aba." The transport of the procession by water is seen below. A funeral barge containing a chest set under a canopy is being towed by a sailing ship, but has also its own steersman and pilot, with one priest (?). The same subject is repeated below, where the barge carries the bier and a small coffer. The embalmer and professional mourning woman sit in the bow. Of the sailing ship only the hind part remains, where a sailor sits on a staging in the high stern, holding the ropes which pull the yard in either direction. Below him is the steersman, who turns the heavy steering oar by means of a tiller. Three passengers are seen in the upper boat.

PLATE VIII. The subject here is divided into five registers, of which the two upper relate, as is stated, to " giving the order for taking stock of the tomb-estate." Three scribes, " trusty before their master," their little vessels of ink or water set on stands before them by their palettes, and a spare pen behind the ear, write busily on tablets. Behind them we see " the bringing of the superintendent of gangs to the great reckoning." The ushers are bringing forward the unhappy foremen who are responsible for the profits made by their departments and who, being determined, like the Egyptian fellah of a few years back, to pay no more than pain or fear extorts from them, have to be prepared by rough treatment for examination at the hands of their lord. Two or three

[1] His figure was at first drawn with arms hanging respectfully, as if Aba was before him ; but this attitude was afterwards corrected to suit the case.
[2] Cf. *Von Bissing, A.Z.* 1889, pp. 75 *seqq.*

[3] The cord by which it is being drawn and which passed through the right hands of the men is almost obliterated.

ushers seem to be needed to reduce the stubborn peasant to a proper appreciation of the position; but as he is pushed to the front he becomes more tractable and at length is seen in a supplicating position before the official, who, whether on his own account or his master's, has only one reply, "Tell me what thou givest."[1] The second row shows the bastinado. First there is a man standing with a stick; a short defaced inscription is before him. Next a peasant is being thrown down and beaten by a man with a short staff. The inscription looks like "forming an embrace." Then follows the punishment of a prostrate man with staves terminating in hands, and a group of a man apparently being roughly raised from the ground by two persons after a severe beating. The obscure inscriptions also probably refer to these groups: "Beating with the *qaat*-stick" is fairly clear; another occurring twice is possibly "Beating is its name, it produces pleasure of heart!"[2] We also see a reference to "the voice of a magistrate." It seems that the delinquent on the ground is being roundly abused, "Thou whom the two houses of his master hate! whom his mistress . . . . . ! whom his master . . . . .!" Lastly we see "the bringing of the superintendent of gangs to the reckoning." The poor wretch, who wears a characteristic apron as in the top row, is being pushed and hauled forward in the most unceremonious way.

In the third register the fullers are occupied with their work regardless of the presence of their master. The scene has evidently little or no connection with the rest of the picture. On the left a man is wringing (?) a roll of thread or cloth. "Binding (?) cloth of beautiful fine linen."[3] Over two men who hold a length of thread or cloth is written, "Folding up a great web." Beneath is a pile of pieces and a chest (?). The next pair of workers seem to be folding a piece of cloth to add to the pile below, the action being described as "Spreading out a great and excellent . . . . ." Over the last pair, who are carrying or stretching a piece of cloth, is, "Fullers of the tomb-estate."

In the lowest register[4] is a row of seven harpists, whose presence and occupation would not, perhaps, to the oriental mind seem incongruous with the judicial scenes shown above. A jar of beer has been provided for them.

A large flint nodule has interfered with the excavation of the N.W. corner of the chamber and the artist has been obliged to provide a small appendix to the scenes both on this and on the N. wall (Plates ix. and xii.). It is repeated on both in an almost identical form, the subject having no connection with the scenes on either wall, but having reference perhaps to the burial place of Henema below. In the upper register offerings are seen piled on tables or contained in jars. Below, the carcase of a goat, which is hanging from the branch of a tree, is being skinned. "Cut it up and make it come," seems to be the injunction, and the answer, "I am doing according to thy pleasure." A man who is described as "A tomb-cook performing his duty," is cutting up meat on a board, while a comrade stirs the joints which are being cooked in a cauldron over a brazier. He remarks, "These are done (?)" In the lowest register the butcher is cutting up the carcase of an ox. One man brings a bowl for the blood,

---

[1] A sign has been omitted in the plate. Read

[2] Possibly Nezem-ab may be the name of the lictor, as in the bastinado scene in the tomb of Mera, where punishment, not execution, is evidently depicted (Daressy, *Mastaba de Mera*, p. 531).

[3] Reading

[4] There are only four registers here, instead of five as elsewhere. The reason for this reduction in the height of the pictures in this part of the tomb is not very obvious.

another holds the heart in his hand and says, " I am offering a great and delicate portion."

NORTH WALL, W. SIDE (Plates xi. and xii.).

Field scenes are here represented, the figure of Aba in the centre dividing the picture into its two natural parts, the tending of animals and the raising of crops. The subdivision of the former subject is characteristic of Egypt. Every princely estate, probably, extended from the Nile to the mountains, thus taking in its proper " hinterland " of waste land or mere, and of desert. We have seen that the fish and fowl to be found in the former were an important item of food-supply : the wild animals found in the desert were so in no less a degree, and were not only hunted for present use but captured alive and fattened in the stalls. Hence while the lower registers here (corresponding to the foreground in the landscape) are occupied with the breeding of domestic animals, the two topmost (farthest) scenes exhibit the fauna of the desert. A deep band coloured red to represent the sand leaves no doubt as to the habitat of the animals. They are represented in their natural state, breeding, grazing, and falling a prey to the king of the desert. Only in the right-hand corner is the hunter seen loosing his hounds or discharging his arrow at the gazelles. The desert was a stockyard rather than a sporting ground to the Egyptian. The top of the picture has suffered greatly, but most of the animals can still be recognized. In front is a lion which with upraised paw majestically crushes an antelope, whose slim legs break under the terrible stroke. A lioness or cheetah follows (as in the tomb at Thebes). A jackal or fox is shown above (i.e. beyond). Two or three oryxes, whose name, *mahez*, is written above them, face to the right, and are preceded by a hedgehog. Above is a fox, followed by two (?) gazelles, one of which, perhaps, is being dragged

down by a dog. Another below seems to be sinking to the ground, pierced through the neck by an arrow, or brought down by the hound behind. In the register below is " a lion bringing down a gazelle," as we read above. Behind, gazelles (of both sexes, as we are informed) are grazing on the scanty herbage. Two wild cattle, " *sma*," two bubales (*shesau*), and two ibexes follow. The latter are incorrectly termed " *henen*," a name elsewhere reserved for the antlered stag. This animal would seem to have been less well known than other kinds, and the name *naa* was not the only one applied to it. (*Ptahhetep*, ii., note p. 16).

A registration of the domestic cattle is being made. "The scribe and steward who is in the heart of his master Sena," writes the total on a tablet, which the convenient rules of Egyptian perspective enable us to peruse. It records " the . . . . . of oxen and goats 32,400," (Plate xxi.). A servant leads forward the finest of the herd, " an ox, great and beautiful." Another assists in the delivery of a calf, while his superior, with ready cudgel, looks on at " the beautiful cow calving." Each of these lower registers opens with a similar group, but behind it in the middle row we are shown two rival bulls in combat, whom the herdsman is " separating " (?). One animal has lifted the other completely from the ground, and the rolling muscles of his thick neck show how capable he is of the feat. " A bull fight " and " a bull covering " are the titles given to this and to the next group. In the lowest register a cow is being milked into a vessel : her hindlegs are tied by way of precaution and the vessel is steadied by a comrade. Finally, goats are seen grazing on herbs or bushes, breeding, walking with their young to new pasture or butting one another, as their nature is. The descriptive column in front of these scenes— " seeing the animals of the desert, and the good tending of cattle for the *Ka* of the *Ha*-prince

. . . . . Aba"—applies to the presence of Aba who leans restfully upon his staff as if prepared for a long review. He wears sandals, probably to protect his feet on the rough field paths. He is accompanied by his wife, his two eldest sons (?), and his brother Zau. The "superintendent of the servants of the *Ka*, who does his lord's pleasure, Usera" approaches with a gift. In front, as if to redeem the picture from appearing a mere reminiscence of life and give it religious significance, is a figure "making incense" by igniting it or stirring it in a dish. He is "the superintendent of the toilette (?)[1] who does his lord's pleasure, Shmaa."

The scenes of agriculture are surveyed by Aba and his wife, who, dressed in their best, sit on a couch side by side. The general inscription is "(Seeing) the ploughing, the gathering of flax, the reaping and carrying and all pleasant festivals of that which belongeth to a day, for the *Ka* of the prince . . . . Aba."[2] The sowing and ploughing evidently occupied the two topmost registers, the gathering of flax is seen in the third, the reaping of wheat in the fourth. The binding of the sheaves and their carriage in rope nets on the backs of asses is shown below, and finally, the stacking of the grain, and the two droves of oxen and of asses which are to tread it out on the threshing-floor.

The appended scene has already been commented on in connection with the west wall, where a fuller form of it appears. On this wall a second appendix (Plate ix.), added below, comprises a list of offerings and a small scene in which Henema sits before the banqueting table, and a servant offers incense. It may be gathered from this that Henema was buried in the vault which opens immediately below.

---

[1] ⌂ has been corrected to ⅍

[2] See the inscription in the tomb of Zau, part ii., plate **vi.**

NORTH WALL, E. SIDE (Plates xiii.—xvi.).

In contrast with the pastoral occupations on the west side, the work of the craftsmen is here shown, whether it is exercised within doors or in the open air, as in the case of the shipbuilders and others. Aba, who wears the stiffened tunic, sits under a light canopy to view the busy scene, which is thus described: "Seeing every kind of labour in the workshop of the artificers, in the hands of every artificer, indoor or outdoor, and the assessment of the handiwork of every artificer by the scribes of his tomb-estate; also the making of the plans of every kind of labour . . . . the Governor of the Residence, Royal Chancellor, sole companion in verity, deserving before Mati through love, Aba."

REGISTERS 1 AND 2.—WORKERS IN STONE AND PRECIOUS METALS—CARPENTERS.

The process of grinding out the interior of large stone vases by means of a kind of centre-bit, is shown first in place as it was earliest among Egyptian achievements. The extraordinary mastery of this art which the prehistoric Egyptians possessed seems reflected in the employment of the picture of this drill as word-sign for "craftsman," stone-working being then confessedly the craft *par excellence*. The tool consisted of an upright rod, weighted near the top with two stones, which were loosely lashed to the stem, and so gave great momentum to the tool when rapidly revolved. The boring was done by a blade with cutting edges at both ends, which was set horizontally across the bottom of the rod, the diameter of the cylinder removed by it varying with the length of the blade employed.[3] The stem, being steadied in the middle by one hand, was revolved by a

---

[3] See BORCHARDT, *Ä.Z.* for 1897, p. 107.

curved crank at the top, or, in later times, by the improved method adopted in our own centre-bits. One workman here is actually using the tool;[1] two others are exhibiting specimens of their handiwork, further examples of which are shown near them. Over three vases in a stand set in front is the inscription, "Making the offering of the craftsman and lector."[2] Over each workman is the word *hemti*, "artificer," or more specifically, "worker in stone." Except on the monuments and in vases of small size, the shapes of the vessels are not familiar; possibly the dimensions are commonly exaggerated in these scenes. From the colour and markings the material seems to be alabaster, which is also otherwise probable. Three other vases in a stand in the lower register appear to belong to this scene. The legend above them seems to be "Polishing hard stone vases, (?)" but no corresponding action is shown. Hard stone was reckoned a precious material, and the dwarfs, therefore, who were in charge of the jewellery, are quite in place here. The action of the two groups appears identical, but over one is the descriptive note, "Threading (?) a collar"[3]; over the other "Furbishing (?) a collar." Collars of various shapes are spread out on stands above.

The remaining part of the two registers is occupied by the workers in wood (Plate xiv.), whether cabinet makers or wood-carvers. The first two groups above represent two men rubbing or planing chests. The inscription informs us that in the one case they are "beating (?) with *sent*[4] on furniture (?) belonging to

the house of the embalmers," and in the other, "beating (?) with *sent* on the coffer of the *sekhem* sceptre . . . ." The workmen are carpenters of the Royal Residence (or of the interior of the house?), and of the tomb-estate respectively. Behind them is a comrade who is fashioning the sceptre above mentioned. In the tomb of Zau it is said to be of electrum. The two next workmen—one of them a "head carpenter"—are engaged on a shrine mounted on runners, which is destined to hold a statue or other article of burial furniture, and be dragged in the funeral procession. The carpenters have slung their adzes over their shoulders, and may be polishing the shrine by hand, but the meaning of the explanatory note is not clear, "Providing a . . . . of *merhet* oil (?)." Further to the left a sculptor gives the final touch with mallet and chisel to the seated statue of a man. "A sculptor chiselling on a statue." His reward, apparently, is awaiting him; for a servant who is squatting behind and holding a bird carefully, says reflectively, "This duck is very fat." Additional scenes from the sculptor's workshop are seen below. The "sculptor Sena" is chiselling a standing statue, which from the hair and pose must be female, despite the colour (red but not flesh-colour). In these tombs an orange approaching red is sometimes used for the flesh-tint of women (*v*. Frontispiece). Next we see "a sculptor working on a lion." The animal both by mane and outline seems to be a male, and not the presentment of Mati, but a lion-headed god may have been associated with her in worship, or the animal may have been sacred to her. A second standing statue, that of a man in close-fitting tunic, appears to be receiving its decoration of paint. "Adorning (?) the face of the statue." Another scribe or painter approaches. Next in order is "a carpenter working on a sedan chair," and behind him "a carpenter working on a staff (?)." The last group shows two "workmen polishing a couch."

---

[1] So in VIREY, *Rekhmara*, plate xiii.

[2] Cf. DARESSY, *Mastaba de Mera*, p. 546.

[3] The person in charge of this department is shown in *L.D.* ii. 60. His titles throw an interesting light on the profession of the ancient artist. See *Sheikh Said*, p. 18, note 3.

[4] Cf. Tomb of Ty, Baedeker, p. 137 (1898 Edition).

REGISTER 3.—WORKERS IN PRECIOUS STONES
AND METALS.

This subject is scarcely separable from the
scenes already described. Here, however, the
raw materials are so valuable that they are
weighed out to the workmen. The balance
has a cross-beam suspended from the top of the
stand, with a board fixed to it at right angles
against which a plummet is hung, so that the
parallelism of the line to this vertical board may
determine the truth of the balance. From each
end of the beam a cord hangs terminating with
a hook, from which bags of material may
easily be suspended. Two men superintend the
weighing. Over one is written "Weighing (lit.
'carrying') metal"; over the other "Seeing
. . . ."

An interesting group follows, which depicts
two men "boring carnelian." The tools and
the blocks of carnelian are doubtless very much
magnified for the sake of clearness. The latter
may only be carnelian beads of the usual size
which are here being pierced, whether by a
turning motion, as we should expect, or by
"jumping" blows, as the action rather suggests.
From the yellow colour of the tool, with blade
and handle, it would seem to be of wood, and
such an instrument might perhaps be employed
if furnished with a hard point or used with
emery powder. The meaning "gravers" may
be hazarded for the signs above. The little
beads or plaques when successfully pierced are
perhaps passed on to their comrades to be
shaped and polished, for we see another pair of
"gravers" (?) "polishing carnelian" by rubbing
it on a block. Another process of metal-
working is seen behind, where two artizans are
"beating electrum." The mass is between
their hands on a block.[1] The man on the right

remarks to his comrade, "Do it on the anvil (?) ; "
to which the reply is made, "It will turn out
well." The more familiar scene of the melting
of the metal follows. Here are six men gathered
round in a circle, a fire being in the midst.[2] Each
is provided with a hollow reed, the end of which
is furnished with a lump of clay to prevent igni-
tion. The six blow-pipes being inserted in the
flame raise it to a sufficiently intense heat to
melt the contents of the crucible (which is not
represented here). The note above describes
the scene as "the melting of metal." The
following sentence, "Ye are about to see (something) good," refers, no doubt, to the food and
jars of beer (?), which an attendant is bringing
to the thirsty smiths.

REGISTERS 4 AND 5.—SHIPWRIGHTS AND SCRIBES.

On the left we see three men trimming the
rough logs into shape with the axe. One is "a
head carpenter." The foremost cries to his
comrade behind "strike hard," to which
admonition he replies, "I am doing what thy
kas desire." The ship for which the curved logs
or planks are destined is on the stocks. Three
carpenters with an overseer (?) are at work with
mallet and chisel. "Lo, I am chiselling," cries
one of them. A fourth, trimming down the end
of the vessel, exclaims, "The axe(?)—it cuts
home ; I am about to see something good." A
second vessel with higher prow and much better
lines is on the stocks to the left. Three
"carpenters chiselling" are seen at work on it ;
a fourth uses the axe. Between the vessels a
gang of four men are transporting a heavy baulk
of timber, roughly squared and trimmed from a
tree trunk. The method is that of the modern

---

[1] Although I could not detect anything in their upraised
hands, the round stones which seem to have been the only
hammers the Egyptians ever possessed, must necessarily
be supplied, as in the corresponding scene in the tomb of
Zau.

[2] The readiness with which the ancient artist resolved a
complex perspective into simple elements, and trusted to
the common sense of his spectators to make the proper
change mentally, is nowhere better exemplified than in this
instance.

shaiyâlin, or porters, in Egypt. The piece of timber is slung from a pole carried on the men's shoulders, so that the weight is well distributed. The men steady the ropes with their hands to prevent any swaying of the load. Presumably the timber is intended for the keel of a ship, or perhaps for a runner on which to drag heavy weights. In the next register the builders are at work upon the baulk. One seems to be trimming off the stumps of branches with an axe,[1] or, it may be, is fashioning the turned up end of a sledge runner (Plate x.), the others are cutting holes for tenons with the haftless copper chisel, which is driven by mallets of a shape familiar to our museums. The "keeper of the bag, Neba," is giving in his report to the scribes while keeping an eye upon his men.[2] The workers are designated "Workmen of the necropolis belonging to the tomb estate, who do the pleasure of the House." One of the workers remarks, "I am working excellently, ye (?) shall see something good." The scribes who deal with the accounts of the workshops sit on the right, facing the busy scene. Good manners, however, demand that one shall turn his head in recognition of his master's presence. Each is provided with pens and tablet, pallet and water-pot, cases or spare tablets, and a chest to hold all. "One who is in the heart of his master," "One who does the pleasure of his master and who is in the heart of his master," "One who does the command of his master," are the honourable, yet condescending, epithets applied to these scribes of the steward.

Register 5.—Family of Aba, etc.

The patriarchal dignity of the deceased is enhanced, as usual, by the presence of his family as well as by the exhibition of his numerous retainers and serfs. His wife and seven sons are here represented, the latter of whom share only four names between them; in face, however, of the many examples of such a practice we may accept the record as true (see p. 12). A scene follows here so inappropriately that it must have been added merely to fill the vacant corner. It really belongs to the series on the W. side of the wall, and represents what was an important branch of farm economy, the keeping of fowl. Here two pens are stocked, the one with cranes, the other with geese, and grain is being thrown to them from a bag by an attendant. In the goose-pen apparently a shelving basin is provided for the birds to swim in. The hollow is indicated by adding two sections of it to the combined plan and elevation of the pen.[3]

East Wall. (Plate vii.)

The scenes on this wall have but little interest, are roughly executed, and are, in addition, in a very bad state of preservation. But the inscriptions are of such value as to make their fragmentary condition a matter of deep regret. The motive of the designer here was essentially biographical, not, however, with the view of merely enumerating the wealth of Aba and the royal favours he had received, but of making them the just ground for maintaining the service of the tomb on a scale commensurate with his rank and wealth, and with the bequests actually made for this purpose. In accordance with this aim the upper third of the wall is occupied by a biographical inscription in six lines which extends over the whole breadth of the wall. It is unfortunate that it was executed in black hieroglyphs, for this pigment, besides being almost invisible on the dark background, seems peculiarly subject to decay. Previous visitors do not seem to have

---

[1] Practical considerations would suggest that the second axe in his hands is a correction of the designer. The rounded top of the mallet may also be an error in the first sketch.

[2] Some one seems to have added the remark, " I am coming," in explanation, perhaps, of the backward glance.

[3] So also in the Tomb of Kagemna, Saqqareh.

remarked the existence of the inscription, and it was only at the third trial that I was able to obtain a copy which seemed worthy of publication (Plate xxiii.).[1] The inscription is divided into two in the middle. On the left-hand side is (1) "[May the king grant] as a grace and Osiris . . . . in all his places the *perkheru* offerings belonging to the *Ha*-prince Aba (?) . . . . (2) Royal Chancellor, Governor of the Residence, Sole Companion, Great Chief of the Thinite(?) nome, Aba. He says, 'I [was] a child who put on the girdle (?) . . . . . [the Majesty of] (3) my lord, King of Upper and Lower Egypt, Merenra . . . . [appointed me?] as *Ha*-prince(?), sole Companion, Great Chief of the *Du-ef* Nome; the Majesty of my Lord, the King of Upper and Lower Egypt [Nefer-Ka-ra?] made me Superintendent of the South.' The Superintendent of [the South] (4) in verity, Aba, says, 'As to any person who shall enter this chamber . . (5) . I was an excellent soul and of good parts; I knew every secret mystery (magic?) of the palace, every . . . of (?) the necropolis . . . . I was (6) one beloved of his father . . . . [praised of] his mother, deserving before the king, deserving before my city-god through love, Aba.'"

On the right-hand is (1) a prayer to Anubis, " . . . . [the West extends] (2) her two hands to him (as?) one deserving before the great God, Lord of Heaven, Aba. He says, . . (3) . . two tomb chambers . . . . (4) of the greatness of my nobility . . . in the *Du-ef* Nome . . Moreover I gave [bread to the hungry], clothing (5) to the naked . . Moreover, I . . . . . . , with seed corn (?) (6) with yoke oxen, with serfs of the tomb estate . . . . . I was one praised . . . ."

Beneath the inscription is a file of female figures, each representing an estate of Aba, and

carrying a bale on her head in token of its productiveness. Only one or two of the estate names can be completely deciphered. The fourth seems to be simply named " Wine ;" the sixth, " Field of . . .;" the eleventh, "The Throne." At the left end of the row Khua (?) offers a bird to his father. Below this procession of estates is an interesting inscription in blue hieroglyphs.

" For the *Ha*-prince, Governor of the Residence, Sole Companion, First after the King, the deserving Aba. I made these as estates, demesnes of eternity (for the tomb?) as a priest by virtue of grace granted by the King (?). The Majesty of my Lord caused to be provided for me . . . . aruras . . . . [he provided?] these with serfs of eternity, filled with oxen, with goats, with asses; [he did this for me] besides the property of my father. Lo, I was governor of a Residence attached to Per-mer (?), (in an estate) of 203 aruras. His Majesty, my lord, gave me [these things] in order to strengthen me."

Below on the right the incidents of the stock-yard are exhibited, and at the bottom of the wall are scenes of ploughing and sowing. The triangle on the right represents presumably a heap of seed corn. Two " scribes of the tomb estate " are watching the work, and are a reminder of the destination of its products. The cattle and cereals which are raised on the estate mentioned above are to furnish the main part of that banquet of the dead which is suggestively pictured above. Aba, who with his wife receives the homage of the properties of the tomb estate as its living master, also sits as the dead proprietor to enjoy the fruits of the property in mortmain. Behind the table are the various provisions stored under shelter (suggested by the papyrus column on the right). The large vase exhibits a design which it is interesting to trace back to its natural source. The artists were accustomed to represent the breccias and granites, of which

---

[1] Only a hand copy of the inscription was possible. The lacunae were measured roughly by eye.

their finest stone vessels were made, by a very exaggerated colouring. A common form of such decoration consists of indiscriminate red and green blotches, the red tending to become diamond-shaped, and to be set in regular rows, the green to become oblong grains, and to be put round the red spots, one on each of the four sides (so in the third vase from the top, Plate xvii.). When the green spots, thus regularly arranged, touched one another, they formed a pattern like that on the vase in Plate xix., and when the diamonds were also made to meet, point to point, the more complicated pattern on Plate vii. resulted, in which the original idea is completely obscured.[1]

THE SHRINE.

Here the essential representations are gathered, those which in a tomb of the simplest type would be the only symbolism employed, if the term can be used of representations that were expected to be thaumaturgic. Of these, the false door, by which the spirit of the dead might enter and depart from the burial vault where the body lay, is of first importance, and it is rather surprising that nothing in the shape of an altar for offerings is provided in front of it. The list of offerings, and the depiction of the banquet of the dead, the presentation of gifts for it, and the performance of the religious ceremonial necessary for their appropriation by the dead, as well as the titles and name by which his identity is assured, are the subjects which obviously were of vital concern, and so find a place here.

WEST WALL. (Plate xvii.) A large part of the wall is occupied by the list of offerings,

---

[1] The black in the pattern represents green; the diamonds are red and the ground drab. The lip of the vase is chequered in black and white.

spaced for 100 entries. As the inscriptions, of the usual type, were very far from being complete, they were not copied. The false door on this wall is carved in the rock, the recess left round the framing being coloured to represent granite. The greater part has been destroyed; what remains shows the usual prayers on Aba's behalf. To the right of this door sits Aba. His titles are inscribed overhead, eight vases of unguents are ranged behind, and beside his chair are articles of personal use. These comprise a coffer, two throw-sticks (?), two batons (?), and three mirrors with lotus-flower handles, one of them being in the hands of a dwarfed attendant. The offerings piled above the door are being consecrated by an embalmer and a Ka-servant of the tomb, Zau, who are purifying the table of offerings, and by the lector, Aba, whose office is "the offering of incense and the reading of the consecrations." To the left of the door are seen the children of Aba, who make meat and drink offerings. They here include his four daughters, Tekhyt, Merab, Henut, and Serezyt, and his sons Khua and Aba, the latter followed by a lector of the same name. Zau is absent, unless the *hen ka zet* above is he.

NORTH WALL. (Plate xviii.) A painted false door is the chief decoration of the wall. It contains the prayers to Osiris and Anubis in the simplest form. The expression, "the *Ha*-prince in verity through love before Anhert," is a welcome variation from the usual formula: the mention of the deity of This was to be expected from the ruler of that nome. On the left of the door are offerings in four tiers. On the right Aba and Henema stand with Serezyt and another daughter, and receive gifts from their sons Zau and Khua and Aba's brother (?) Zau. It will be remembered that the opening into the long passage which slopes down to the burial vault is immediately beneath this scene. The line of titles given at the top of this plate is written in on the rebate over the entrance to the shrine.

EAST WALL. (Plate xix.) The list of offerings (ninety-nine entries) again occupies a conspicuous place. The representation is very similar to that on the opposite wall, but the false door is replaced by a banqueting table and a lavish pile of offerings, in which a magnificent bowl again appears (cf. Plate vii.). Aba's pet here is a female monkey, which has been provided with a basket full of fruit. She has been dressed with bracelets, anklets, and collar like a woman. The blue (to represent bluish-gray?) on head and body marks the colour of the animal's hair, and its separation from the red of the face, hands, and feet. The gifts which the servants bring in the two upper registers are described as "(the tribute) of his tomb estate for the *Ka* of Aba." One of the figures represents "the chief scribe and superintendent of *Ka*-servants, who does the pleasure of his master, Rensi son of Aba." The lustration and the reading of magic texts by the lector Aba goes on as before, accompanied here by acts of adoration or prayer from two other celebrants, and the mysterious ceremony in which a priest walks away trailing a staff (?) on the ground. The sons, Zau and Khua, and the second Zau (?) offer gifts.

TOMB OF [hieroglyphs] HETEPNEB.

No. 2.   PLATES XXI. AND XXIII.

The tomb was hewn in a low ledge of rock which is now worn away. The chamber is destroyed to the foundations, except at the back where the N. wall is preserved and a little of the roof. In the E. wall is a small false door. On the N. is a shrine-recess, the floor of which is occupied by a shallow pit, from which a narrow passage to the N. leads to a small vault. The N. wall of the shrine is occupied by a painted tablet framed within a border. On the right hand side are jars and food-offerings: on the left Hetepneb sits before a banqueting table, over which is written a prayer for thousands of various viands, "for the *Ka* of Hetepneb." Above his head is the following inscription in green hieroglyphs :—

"May the King grant as a grace and Anubis on his hill (grant) his fair burial in a chamber (of the necropolis), as (to) one deserving before Osiris in all his seats, the Companion, First after the King, possessing (?)[1] thousands of things of his own, with (or, 'superintendent of') herds of goats, one deserving before . . . . who does the pleasure of his lord, deserving before Mati, through love, Hetepneb."

On the E. side of the recess the figures of Hetepneb and his wife are visible, the latter with hands upraised. Her name may be [hieroglyphs].

TOMB OF [hieroglyphs] (?) UHA.

No. 14.   PLATES XXI. AND XXIII.

The exterior is finished off with smoothed jambs and a long lintel band. The walls of the interior are well squared. Three galleries for burial are hewn in the E. wall about two feet above the level of the floor, and two in the N. wall. A gallery below floor level also runs to the W. under Tomb 15. The pit is only a few feet deep, and merely enlarges slightly below.

The memorial is on a small plaster tablet in the middle of the W. wall. On the left a female (?) figure sits facing a banqueting table piled with viands. The inscription above seems to refer to a *Ḥa*-prince and Governor of the Residence, but this is very doubtful. No name is legible. On the right a larger male figure stands facing the table and holding a staff in his left hand. There is a prayer above for *perkheru* gifts "for the sole companion Uha (?)."

---

[1] Mr. P. Newberry reads [hieroglyphs].

TOMB OF ⬤𝄞𝄞⌣ TEKHYT.

No. 16.   PLATES XXI AND XXIII.

The exterior is fashioned like that of tomb
No. 14. The chamber within is hewn with
some care, but the partition wall on the E. has
given way. The three shafts are full of *débris*.

The memorial is on a small plaster tablet on
the N. wall, and is framed in a border of rect-
angles. On the right a lady sits before a
banquet table, on which viands and vases are
arranged. Overhead is the inscription in blue
hieroglyphs: "The sole Royal Ornament, deserving before Mati, Tekhyt."

TOMB OF 𝄞〰𝄡𝄞〰 SENBSEN.

No. 28.   PLATE XXIII.[1]

This tomb was hewn in the secondary ledge
of rock, and in consequence the E. chamber is
entirely unroofed and the front part of it
destroyed. The large chamber to the right,
which is probably part of the same tomb, retains
its roof, but is uninscribed. The floor is not
visible.

Only a few fragments of the representations,
which seem to have covered the N. wall of the
ruined chamber, can be made out, and even those
obscurely. The lower part of a large male
figure is seen on the right with the end of a
vertical column of hieroglyphs, reading, " deserving before Anubis, Senbsen." On the other side
of an immense jar is a female figure (his wife?),
"one deserving before Mati, Mistress of Aakemt(?),
Senuyt." In front of her again is a banquet
table (green stand, red top, green and red reeds
alternately), beside which is written the prayer
for food and clothing. Above it is a female figure
to which the name Senuyt is attached, and who is

---

[1] By an oversight this tomb was not measured : the plan
on Plate I. is from memory only.

therefore probably a daughter. Beyond the
table is another female figure named Mererut,
who holds a lotus flower in her hand. A column
of hieroglyphs in front again gives the name
Aakemt as the seat of worship of Mati, a reading
which has a clear confirmation in a tomb of the
northern group (Vol. ii. Plate xxi.).

TOMB OF ⬤𝄞⌣ MERUT.

No. 33.   PLATES XXII. AND XXIII.

The space round the doorway is smoothed,
but the lintel (square) is within the entrance.
The tomb (wrongly numbered 34 in Plate xxii.)
is now of very considerable size, but the spacious
inner chamber may be a later construction, as
it is separated from the ante-room by pilasters
and an architrave. The large room has a shrine-
recess in the back wall, and in the uneven floor
are thirteen shafts, all now full, or nearly so.
In the N.E. corner is an unquarried mass. The
ante-room also has a shaft, empty for seven
feet, in front of a false door, a part of the inscriptions of which has been destroyed by the
cutting of a niche. On the E. wall are three
small niches, arched and plastered. The ceiling
is lowered by a few inches halfway back and the
W. wall also shows signs of an alteration of plan
at this point.

The inscription is on the false door in the S.
wall. The lintel contains the prayer for all
varieties of food and clothing in thousands, and
the designation " one deserving before Mati,
mistress of Aakemt (?), one who does that which
is commended, Merut." On the lintel Merut is
seen with her hands upraised in blessing (?)
before the table of offerings. A prayer to Osiris
is on the other side. On the left jamb is a
prayer to Anubis; on the right is the more
unusual prayer to the king alone. Merut is
described as " beloved of her father and her
mother;" the drum and the tablet seem to have
recorded her surname.

Tomb of ⌇⊛⌽⌉ Nefer-tep-wa (?).

No. 41.   Plates XXI. and XXIII.

This, with Tomb 40, lies high up, near the summit of the hill. The excavation of the low slope which was necessary in order to obtain a façade has formed a large court, shared by the two tombs. The façade of each is vertical and plain. The floor within is not visible. The subsidiary chambers open out of the small room, that to the N. being reached by a low passage of some length. Above the entrance to this is a plastered tablet on which a list of offerings is written in faded black ink. Below it is a figure in a long robe, holding a staff and the *kherp* sceptre, accompanied by illegible green hieroglyphs. A pit in the S.E. corner leads into a lower room, half passage, half chamber, which extends eastward, narrowing and descending by two steps before becoming blocked by rubbish.

The inscription is on a small plastered tablet on the E. wall. A male figure, clothed in a simple tunic, is seated on a chair on the left; a column in front gives his name and titles as "the Sole Companion, the deserving Nefer-tep-wa (?)." A prayer to the king alone on his behalf runs overhead. In front of him is a standing female figure, "the royal noblewoman Sekhatusen (?)."

Tomb of ⌇⌇⌒⌒⌒⊛⌒⌐🦅 Nefer-nef-khetu (?).

No. 42.   Plates XXI. and XXIII.

The façade is merely smoothed and is vertical. The interior is well laid out, but the surface of the walls is rough. There is an arched niche in the N. wall. The three shafts are nearly full of rubbish; that in the S.W. corner expands to the W. a little below floor level. On the W. wall a space, three feet by five, is slightly recessed, smoothed, thinly plastered and inscribed

with a list of offerings. Beneath this the deceased is seen seated, facing to the right, and before him is another figure in a long garment. The inscription over them is illegible.

A tablet on the E. wall, similar but smaller, is inscribed in red and green inks. Here the deceased sits on the right, facing a table of offerings. Opposite him on the other side is a standing figure with *kherp* sceptre and staff. The prayer above reads, "May the king grant as a grace the *perkheru* offerings which belong to Nefer-nef-khetu, beloved of his father and mother, praised of his brother, deserving before the great god."

The smaller tombs in this necropolis fall very far indeed behind those of the nomarchs, and suggest no advanced rank and no great amount of material prosperity; yet we may be deceived. The "Sole Royal Ornament, Tekhyt," of Tomb 16, may well be identified with the daughter of Aba; and if this tiny chamber, eight feet square, in which her *Ka* could not have stood upright if it shared the limitations of mortality, was the "eternal home" assigned to a princess while her brother was hewing out and decorating his spacious hall, and if the tiny tablet was considered her sufficient memorial, we must be prepared to grant that the other tombs and caves may have been the burial places of high officials. As it is, the inscribed tombs seem all to have belonged to Sole Companions at least, and it would not be surprising, therefore, if Hetepneb spoke truth in describing himself as owner of "a thousand cattle (?) of his own," and if Tomb 14 belonged to the governor of a residence. Merut, who reached the distinction of a false door, can scarcely have been less than the prince's daughter of that name, and Senbsen can hardly be estimated at less than princely dignity. When this is so, it cannot be expected that the rank and file of Aba's subjects ever thought of a rock tomb for themselves, a deduction which may help towards a solution of the puzzling problem as to what population is represented by the comparatively small cemeteries which are found in Egypt. Did the mode of burial of the general population involve the disappearance of their remains, or did this follow as the result of the scant courtesy they met with at the hands of succeeding generations? Perhaps some day the data will be reached by which we shall be able to estimate the population of the district which interred its dead at this spot; if so, the separate description of these uninteresting burial places will not have been useless.

III.—THE NOMARCH AND THE NOME

In such a volume as this, the plates constitute the really valuable part. Through them, if they are only reliable and complete, an ancient document, the future value of which not the most foreseeing can estimate, is snatched from immediate danger of decay or destruction. But after sufficient care has been bestowed upon the copy and some attempt made to interpret it so far as present knowledge permits, it will still be expected by many that something should be done to place the facts thus chronicled in living connection with the time and circumstance. The learned indeed may wish that such attempts were left to the few who can claim competence, and these in turn would often relegate the task to the more convenient season when Egyptology shall have accumulated and indexed its *data*. But perhaps the impulse to make history, even, at times, by paths of hazard, is not unjustified. It serves to remind the worker that he is dealing, not with a dead body of fact, but with a record of life. His hypotheses may prove the rough means by which vitality is maintained in what seems lifeless; until, quickened by a fitting environment, it asserts itself again as a piece of living history.

We scarcely need the cry of bereavement which rises in the midst of the formal prayers and conventional phrases in the tomb of Zau, to remind us that these ancient nomarchs were men about whom a whole world of affection and dependence, love and hatred, gathered. There are indications also that they played a part in the stirring political events of their time, though they may not have had the good fortune to be sent, like Una or Herkhuef, on great expedi-

tions for the king, which, whether peaceful or warlike, were full of adventure and romance, and success in which brought everlasting fame, as well as immediate reward to their leaders. There does exist, at least, a chapter of history in which we may attempt to include the lives of these princes. For they lived when the national life was in culmination, and has left us fuller records than at any other period of the Ancient Kingdom. The biographies of the two great officials named above in themselves contain a picture of the public life of the time, which serves as a background to throw into greater distinctness the careers of other office-bearers of the period. On the other hand, the picture of private life which has been put together from records of earlier date receives many vivacious touches and considerable amplification from contemporary tombs, and not least from those of this necropolis where flat painting gave an opportunity for detail which sculpture had not afforded. Finally, something may be learnt of the modes in which men of this distant age thought, from the religious faith and the burial customs which the inscriptions disclose.

We have in this necropolis the record of eight princes of the nome with the title of " Great Chief." Five of these were buried on the more northern site, and almost certainly were the predecessors—probably the immediate predecessors—of Aba and his descendants. The tombs of that group, however, are so wrecked, that it is very improbable that the names of all the princes buried there have been preserved. Probably one or two more tombs at least belong to men of that rank. This would take us half way back through the Vth Dynasty. There is much less likelihood of failure in the record of a prince buried in the southern tombs ; for the few large chambers which are now blank are intact, yet show no trace of former inscriptions. The tomb of Senbsen, however, may well have belonged to one of princely rank.

Neglecting this, we have in the southern group three members of one family, who in succession received from the king the office of Great Chief of the Nome. They are Aba, his son Zau-Shmaa, and the latter's son Zau, who was buried in one tomb with his father. M. Maspero, who had only Professor Sayce's erroneous report before him, concluded that Zau-Shmaa was the elder and that his son Aba was to be identified with the owner of the neighbouring tomb.[1]

The reverse is now seen to be the case. By both name and surname Zau-Shmaa is identified as the son of Aba. Additional proof of this order of descent is afforded by the biographical inscription of Aba, which shows that he derived his early honours from Merenra. Had Zau-Shmaa been the earlier of the two, he must have fallen in the reign of Pepy I. and could not then have held the priesthood of the Pyramid of Pepy-Neferkara.

This line of rulers, by abandoning the burial-place of previous princes, and hewing out in a new site tomb-chambers, which in size and quality of decoration put to shame all previous attainments in the nome, announces itself as a new family. This is also shown by the names, which are almost entirely fresh. But a much more astonishing feature is that these three princes are Great Chiefs, not only of the Du-ef Nome in which they are buried, but also of the Thinite (VIIIth) Nome, a district of importance in which both Abydos, the seat of the

worship of Osiris, and This, the early capital of the kingdom, were situated. It is evident too, from the prominence which is repeatedly given to the latter nome in the lists of Aba's honours, that the prince was much more proud of his connection with the Thinite Nome than with the XIIth Nome, in which notwithstanding he probably resided during his lifetime, and at any rate was ultimately buried. In the case of Zau-Shmaa this peculiar preference is less noticeable, and it is no longer shown by his son, who in his long inscription on plate xiii. only mentions the chieftainship of the Du-ef Nome. If therefore Aba, the head of the family, had hereditary rights in either nome, his connection would seem to have been with the Nome of This.

Evidence in support of this view comes from that nome itself, as M. Maspero (loc. cit.) has pointed out; and though it is considerably weakened by the change in order of succession, it is scarcely to be abandoned. It is of great importance, as it connects the princes of this nome closely with the royal family. The name Zau is of very rare occurrence.[2] When it is found, therefore, as the name of a member of an important family of the time, it is natural to identify the families if not the individuals ; for most Egyptian personal names in early times have a very narrow range. Mariette found at Abydos the stela of one Zau,[3] who there informs us that he was the son of Khua and his wife Nebt, and the brother-in-law of Pepy-Meryra; his two sisters having been married to that monarch and borne him the two sons who

---

[1] Recueil de Travaux, xii. p. 68.

[2] From [hieroglyphs] "a staff." The determinative is written upright, but there seem to be exceptions to this practice. (Vol. ii. plates vii. and ix.) For occurrences of the name see Ä. Z. 1900, p. 65, where a palanquin-bearer is named " Zau, the Bedouin," and MARIETTE, Abydos, i. plate ii.

[3] Gizeh, 1431.

succeeded him, Merenra and Neferkara.[1] Zau-Shmaa cannot be identified with this namesake of his, since we have seen him to be the son of Aba. But we can well believe that Aba was a son of the Zau of Abydos, and that it was in loyalty to the family traditions that he named his eldest son Zau after his father, and his second son Khua after his grandfather. If so, Zau of Abydos had in addition a son named like himself, for a brother of that name is depicted in the tomb of Aba (Plates iii., xi.).[2]

The house of Aba, then, seems to have sprung from Abydos.[3] The titles given to Khua on the stela of his son show him to have been an *Erpa Ha* prince, and his son succeeded him in this hereditary rank, adding to it the highest honours. If, then, Aba was the son of this Zau, he would inherit the title " hereditary prince "

by birth in the VIIIth Nome, and not by connection with the XIIth. But later it seems to have passed to a collateral branch of the family at Abydos, for we find it claimed (in Neferkara's reign ?) by another Khua (also married to one Nebt, yet not identifiable with the father of the Queen) and descending to his son Ada.[4] The rulership of the *Du-ef* Nome may have come to Aba by right of marriage. One of the last rulers buried in the northern necropolis was a prince Rahenem, whose wife also bore the same name. His tomb preserves no memory of a daughter ; yet, as Aba's wife was so named, there is much likelihood that she belonged to this house, and that it was through marriage with this heiress that Aba acquired the claim to have the rulership of the *Du-ef* Nome assigned to him by the king. It is very unfortunate that the biographical notice in Aba's tomb is so badly preserved. It probably informed us in whose reign he " put on the girdle " (*i.e.* emerged from childhood), what his rank was before King Merenra (as it seems) made him *Ha*-prince (?) Sole Companion and Great Chief of the *Du-ef* Nome, and what further dignities Neferkara conferred upon him. Teta does not seem to have made his power felt far from the capital, but Pepy I. was wise or powerful enough to remedy this weakness, and his marriage into a family of Abydos not improbably had a political end in view.[5] It is significant, at any rate, that it is followed in the next reign by the assignment of the nomarchy of This to princes who seem to have

---

[1] Both sisters are named Meryra-ankhnes, having, perhaps, been renamed on marriage. One became the mother of Merenra, and may have died before her sister married the king and gave birth to Neferkara, who must have been considerably younger. This new interpretation of an important monument is due to Dr. BORCHARDT, who communicated to me his belief that the two figures of the queen must represent two separate persons, in face of the claim which Zau makes to be " their brother," and has also kindly permitted me to make use of his discovery. It is certainly the most straightforward reading of the inscription, and must long ago have found acceptance, but for the natural bias against the practice involved—a practice, however, which was common in Egypt, and of which these tombs give evidence, perhaps for this very family. The inscription in the Wady Maghara (L. *D.* ii. 116), which confirms the birth of Neferkara from Meryra-ankhnes, gives only a negative testimony by its silence regarding the birth of Merenra ; for Neferkara was concerned only with his own descent.

[2] The alternative is possible, therefore, that this brother is to be identified with the Zau of the stela, making Aba another son of Khua and Nebt and a brother-in-law of Pepy I. But besides that this makes Aba rather early in date, he would surely, had this been the case, have announced his near relationship to the Queens, as Zau of Abydos has done ; the latter also would have been given his high titles in Aba's tomb.

[3] The names Shmaa, Ada, Beba, Pepyna, Pepyankhnes, which occur in these tombs, seem all to be names of family connections at Abydos. The names of the daughters are mostly peculiar, perhaps local.

[4] MARIETTE, *Cat. d'Abydos*, pp. 86-88. The name on the stela (Gizeh, 1578) is plainly N.k.b.t., as De Rougé perceived. The stela of Ada (Gizeh, 1575) shows, however, that this must be a sculptor's error.

[5] It may have been both custom and policy that the King as King of Upper Egypt should marry an heiress of the South, and *vice versâ*. Compare the titles and . De Rougé, *Six Premières Dynasties*, p. 133.

been non-resident. In doing so Merenra was probably carrying out an earlier policy of his father. Who preceded Aba as Great Chief of the Thinite Nome is not known; but as Pepy I. had married into the princely family, we may be sure that the office was in friendly hands. The trial of the Queen Amtes suggests treasonable cabals against which that king had to contend, and his selection of his proved servant Una to investigate the case, rather than the high officials to whom it should properly have fallen, speaks more for the precaution of the king than for the security of his position. His great military expeditions to the South would demand a base of operations and supply much nearer than Memphis, and by lending new importance to the South country, render it necessary that all provincial rulers should fully recognise the power of the throne. In the case of the VIIIth Nome, Merenra, while complying with hereditary claims and even seeming to increase the power of the nomarch by doubling the sphere of his rule, may in reality have kept in his own hands the control of the most important province by virtually banishing its nomarch to the other district under his sway, the remote and less important *Du-ef* Nome. It is quite conceivable however that the reason for the double nomarchy was one more flattering to the loyalty of Aba. Whether because he was regarded as a friend or as a danger to the state, his marriage to the heiress of the *Du-ef* Nome seems to have been permitted, and the rulership of that province conferred upon him by Merenra. Then, later, when the rulership of the VIIIth Nome fell vacant, or when Aba's fidelity to the crown and acquiescence in this arrangement had been well assured, Neferkara bestowed this dignity also upon him. It would be quite natural that the latter title, which was considered due by birth to the hereditary prince, should be more esteemed by him than the chieftainship which he acquired through his wife. It is equally natural that his son, and still more his grandson, should acquiesce in their absence from Abydos and feel at home in the province in which they had so long been domiciled.

Whatever may have been the motive for Aba's removal to the XIIth Nome, there is no

GENEALOGY OF THE FAMILY OF ABA.

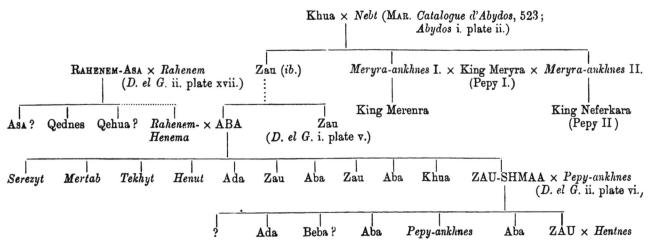

N.B. Broken lines represent hypothetical connections.
Names in small capital letters are those of nomarchs of the XIIth Nome.
Names in large capitals are those of nomarchs of both nomes.
Names in italics are those of females.

sign of rebellion, but, on the contrary, of close understanding between the throne and his family.[1] He may have felt so united to the fortunes of his royal cousins as to have agreed to their policy; not less readily, we may believe, if, though his right of rule in the VIIIth Nome was nominal, his right of revenue was allowed. This acquiescence by the family is exhibited in their acceptance of the tutelary goddess of the XIIth Nome. Aba alone permits himself a solitary assertion of his loyalty to Anhert, the god of the home of his fathers, from whose jurisdiction he had passed, but whom he, nevertheless, desired to acknowledge.

In endeavouring to gain some further light on the activities in which Aba engaged, it is natural to turn to the list of honours and offices which are mentioned with wearisome iteration in this, as in all large tombs. But there is much in these lists that calls for caution in their use. Besides that they often seem negligently drawn up, we scarcely yet have the means of gauging their real significance, of separating empty designations from important offices, giving to antiquated titles their real meaning and ranging the indicated honours in a true scale of worth. Some of the offices may have been passed through and left behind, though the conservative Egyptian mind clung to the mention of them; others represented duties which belonged *ex officio* to the higher office and were not separately granted. We may believe, for instance, that Aba had had charge at some time of the granaries, the game-preserves, the custom-houses of the district; or, with more probability, that as *Ha*-Prince or Great Chief of the nome

he was the official head of these departments and responsible for them. As Chief Lector and Chief Priest, he had left behind, we must suppose, the grades of Lector and Secondary Priest; yet these also are duly chronicled. His Chieftainship probably carried with it the religious office of Chief Lector, and such ecclesiastical duties as are suggested by the titles " Director of every divine office," " Scribe of the accounts of the god," as well as the mysterious priestly titles the form of which depended on the local cult. The priesthood of the king's pyramid may be taken to be a special mark of royal favour. The Chieftainship or Hereditary Princedom probably also carried with it by customary right the ancient judicial titles 𓀀 𓊖 and 𓏏 𓊮. But the real judge-ship seems at this time to have been wisely separate from the executive power of the prince, for the high judicial office 𓉐 𓃭 𓃀 is one of the few that are not assigned to Aba or his sons.

Without fuller knowledge of provincial politics in Egypt, it is not easy to fix the exact significance of this office of the Great Chief or Nomarch. It has not yet been found for the nomes of Lower Egypt, and it has hitherto been considered a creation of the VIth Dynasty; but if the priority of the princes of the northern tombs holds good, the office must run far back into the Vth Dynasty. It represents perhaps an attempt of the king to regulate and unify the government of the upper provinces, and to counterbalance the patriarchal power of the *Erpa* prince by this administrative office of the nomarch, resting on a central government and only amalgamated with heredi-tary claims by the free favour of the king. But it was more easy to introduce the title and office than to gain for it proper recognition from princes or people. Like all Orientals, the people preferred the capricious but personal rule of the prince of the land, whose rule was by birthright,

---

[1] The stela of Zau, of Abydos, seems to present the same situation. For, though the record that he made his grave at Abydos " for love of the Nome in which I was born of the Royal Lady Nebt," might be the words of an exile, he is not afraid to boast of his high lineage or of the favour which three kings in succession had shown him, and upon which he relied for exceptional burial honours.

to the blessings of organized officialdom, whose root was in the distant capital. The prince in his tomb boasted first and foremost, not of the nomarchy, but of his birthright; and many an antiquated and empty dignity took precedence of it in his list of honours.[1] Not that he was disloyal to the king or the system; but the title had no personal attachment. It was conferred on him, not born with him, and as a less personal quality had less power to establish his identity in the tomb.

The scenes on tomb walls rarely contain anything in the way of direct personal reminiscence. Yet the introduction of an unusual representation, or the unusual elaboration of a familiar subject, may be the reflection of character and personal achievement. Such exceptional treatment is found in the scene on plate viii., which represents Aba's strict and personal administration of the estate, as also in the representation of the workshops of the residence (plates xiii. to xvi.). The *Du-ef* Nome was probably very much more rural, and less in touch with the capital, than the nome in which Abydos was situated. The small renown of any town in it in ancient days confirms this, and the great advance in tomb decoration made by the family of Aba appears to bear witness to more than an influx of wealth. Aba would thus bring with him from Abydos lessons of that which organization and training can do to make a large landed estate yield wealth to its owner, with the amenities and artistic luxury which wealth can procure. However unpleasantly Oriental the summary discipline used on the official underlings on his estate may appear to us, it may have been extremely wholesome for peasants who had been accustomed to go their lax way. It would be true to human nature if these little

"foremen of gangs" were themselves the most oppressive taskmasters; and even if the rule of Aba was far from benevolent it might yet be a beneficial exchange. This new sight of the palanquin of the nomarch swiftly carrying him here and there in the land was no doubt very distasteful; but it was probably a great benefit to the province that the strong hand of Aba should be felt throughout its borders.

We are justified in putting so favourable an interpretation on this scene because of the companion picture. This depiction of the local handicrafts is so full and betrays so exceptional an interest as to convince us of the capacity of the prince for his task, and suggests that his settlement in this nome may have been an acknowledgment by the king of his powers of organization rather than of his ability to make mischief in Abydos. High attainment in handicrafts, and the production of beautiful objects with tools adapted to the task, is perhaps the test of material civilization, and the promise of what is still higher: nor is the maxim any less applicable because in Egypt a large part of the output was destined to furnish the home, not of the living, but of the dead. This patronage of crafts seems to have been more than the caprice of a wealthy prince, who imported artificers from outside to keep him supplied with luxuries.[2] As the inscription shows, the workshops were highly organized; the material was weighed out to each workman, and entered in the books of the department; and head men were kept to supply the craftsmen with new designs, or arrange their work for them. Too little is known of the organization, whether feudal or otherwise, under which the Egyptian craftsman turned out such finished work. The expression "workmen of the interior and exterior" may mean those who labour in the work-rooms of the residence, and those whose occupation takes them into the

---

[1] So at Sheikh Saïd in the tomb of Uau and frequently here. This statement would have to be discounted if it could be shown that the last place on the list next to the personal name was also a place of honour.

[2] The designer of the tomb of Zau seems at any rate to have been settled in the district.

D

open air. But it may possibly mean those who
work for the palace as distinguished from such
as work for their own hand outside it. In this
case the interest of the nomarch would be the
more meritorious. The province probably
afforded ample material for manufacture:
alabaster for vases, wood for statues, furniture
and boat-building, and perhaps metals also.[1]
Not, indeed, that these resources had been
hitherto altogether neglected: workers in metal
are depicted also in a tomb of the northern
cemetery.

It is impossible even to conjecture how long
Aba ruled over the *Du-ef* Nome. The curious
indifference to the past which the Egyptians
showed, and which was perhaps due to their
strong interest in the future, prevented them
from making any statement as to the age of the
deceased at burial. The element of biography,
too, entered so little into tomb records, that
these princes rarely left any indication at what
age they occupied the heritage of their fathers.
Honour was still a concern of those who had
passed from visible life, but not the accidents by
which it had been attained.

Even had the biographical inscription of Aba
been preserved intact, it is hardly likely to have
afforded additional evidence as to his character
or benevolence, attested as it is by himself alone
and couched in the current phrases. But the
presence of an inscription of this kind does
afford some guarantee that this prince acknow-
ledged the ideals of character and of princely
duty to which the best spirits of the nation had
attained. Whatever else it may imply, the
double nomarchy is a tribute to his personal
ability, and possibly also to his zeal in administration; which, if it fulfilled the ancient
Egyptian estimate of good government, must
have been actively paternal and solicitous for
the weak. The other inscription on the east

wall points out the further favours granted by
the king to Aba, not by way of honour and
enrichment among the living, but in the matter
of burial equipment and suitable provision for
the service of the tomb when he should be laid
in it. It bears additional evidence, if that were
necessary, to the cordial relations between
prince and king. The mention of his father's
property is also interesting, corroborating the
evidence of Aba's high birth. Unfortunately,
the faded estate-names give us no clue to the
locality in which the property was situated.

The consideration of this inscription as
evidence of the king's prerogative in connection
with the burial of his subjects is reserved for the
second volume, when we shall meet with a more
explicit declaration of Zau on the same subject.
The two tombs promise to give very valuable
aid towards removing the mystery from the
seten dy hetep formula and practice.

THE NOME. Apart from the record now
afforded by these tombs, hardly anything is
known of the history of the XIIth Nome in
ancient times, and very little even at a later
date. The lists have suffered mutilation at this
point in some cases, but we learn from them
that its capital was named Net-
ent-bek "the city of the Hawk," or
Per-hor-nub" "the city of the golden Hawk."
Besides the worship of Horus in this form,
there was also, according to the lists, the cult of
Mati, a form of Hathor. Mati, as these tombs
have shown, is the deity who was especially
reverenced in the nome in the time of the
Ancient Kingdom.[2] In Roman times a Pretorian
cohort of the Lusitani was quartered at the
capital of the province, and a relic of this
occupation was discovered by Mr. Harris in the
village of Deir el Gebrâwi. It is a black stone
inscribed with a dedication of the camp to its

---

[1] DUMICHEN, *Geschichte d. alt. Ägyptens*, pp. 171-3.

[2] For an early mention of the deity see L. D. ii. 80 *b*.

deities, and it is now built into the interior of the village church. There was another Roman camp at Isiu, which may also lie within the borders of the nome towards the south.

The site of the capital has not been determined. The name of the most important village at present, Ebnub or Banub, has an Egyptian sound, and if it be taken to represent a shortened form of Per (hor) nub, may indicate the ancient site. A branch of the river still passes close to it, so that the situation would be very suitable. It is indeed far from the necropolis; but, as its present inhabitants still bury at this very spot, it is evidently regarded as most suitable for the purpose, or as consecrated by age-long custom. The power of this latter motive may remain unweakened even by the two enormous breaches in sympathy made by Islâm and Christianity : it is curious that the Copts still bury beneath the heights of the southern necropolis, the Mohammedans opposite the northern tombs. If Ebnub is not the site of the ancient capital, the latter must be looked for nearer the two places of burial, and perhaps at Deir el Gebrâwi itself. The Roman camp, judging by remains opposite the village, was situated here, and perhaps one of its important duties would be to watch the mouth of the Wady which enters the hills a little to the west of the northern necropolis, and is the only road northwards on the east bank. It emerges from the hills into the plain of Tell el Amarna, and is a route still used by drovers. The name of the Old Kingdom town, or perhaps only of the sanctuary of Mati, is gained from the tombs of Deir el Gebrâwi, where the goddess is repeatedly referred to as its mistress. It is usually written merely by a vase of the *des* type, set within an oval enclosure fortified by four or six bastions. But on two or three occasions the name appears spelt out as 𓀭 Aakemt, followed by the above determinative (Tomb of Senbsen, plate xxiii. and vol. ii., plate xxi.). It also appears in what seems to be a shortened form 𓀭 "Aket." [1]

It is possible that in later times the worship of Mati, overshadowed by the worship of the Hawk, had become an unimportant cult, and that in consequence of this decline her sanctuary had disappeared, or so diminished as no longer to have an independent name. Perhaps even the male and female deities had been originally worshipped together in forms which represented a terrifying rather than a mild influence; the one as the Victorious Hawk, the other as the Lioness. Or it may be that the male companion of Mati the lioness was Mahesa the desert lion, who was certainly worshipped in the district immediately to the south.

---

[1] In a list of the places of burial of relics of the gods it is said that a finger of the god Hapi was buried at Per-hor-nub in a jar (𓀭). This legend may be of very ancient date, and the source of the determinative for the sanctuary (BRUGSCH, *Dict. Géog.* p. 1359). But the legend may also be derived from the determinative. A phonetic value for the latter may perhaps be found through the title 14 (p. 8), which has a tempting resemblance to the name of the sanctuary, and heads the list of religious offices.

APPENDIX

The Tomb of Aba at Thebes.[1]

The tomb of Aba in the Assasif at Thebes is of a very different character from that of his name-sake at Deir el Gebrâwi. It consists of an extensive and elaborate suite of underground chambers excavated in the rock and reached by an open stairway. This descends in a southerly direction to a small ante-chamber, the walls of which are adorned with sculptures. A doorway on the right leads hence into a larger sculptured chamber, the roof of which was formerly supported by two square pillars, probably with Hathor-head capitals. It is on the south wall of this room that the scenes are found which have been borrowed from Deir el Gebrâwi. From the north wall a doorway leads into a third chamber, the walls of which are decorated as before.[2] The tomb is continued to the north, first by a hall supported on six columns and then, to the north and west, by a suite of smaller rooms which are undecorated. In the hall, also, only the columns are inscribed.

The tomb, though magnificent in construction, cannot lay claim to great excellence in the execution of its sculpture. A part of the decoration, including the large figures of the deceased, is in high relief, and the work is here

of considerable merit. But the smaller scenes are in *relief en creux*, and though in many parts a certain amount of care has been bestowed upon them, and detail introduced, they cannot claim to rank as works of art. All the hiero-glyphs are incised and coloured blue.

Aba, whose name is spelt indifferently ⌐⌐⌐, ⌐⌐⌐ and ⌐⌐⌐, was an *Erpa-ha* prince, Royal Chancellor of Psammetichus I. (B.C. 664—610) and Chief Steward of the queen Netaqert.

The south wall of the second chamber is occupied by two scenes. On the right hand Aba sits under a canopy and is entertained by various dancers, musicians, &c., who are ranged in five registers in front of him. On the left hand Aba stands, surveying the artificers of the tomb-estate, who are engaged in making funeral furniture of all kinds. These also are arranged in five registers; a sixth, which extends from end to end of the wall under both scenes, is occupied by men and women representing the estates of Aba, who bring tribute to their master.

A comparison of the left half of the wall (Plates xxiv. and xxv.) with plates xiii. to xvi. of the present work will at once show the reason for its reproduction here.[3] The coincidence alike of the groups and the inscriptions is so

---

[1] For a plan and general treatment of the tomb the reader is referred to the publication of Father Scheil, "*Tombeaux Thébains*," pp. 624, *seqq.*, to which the author is also indebted for such information as was not to be gained from his own partial examination of the tomb.

[2] Scheil, no doubt on sufficient grounds, describes the room as an open court with covered gallery. At present the roof is almost entirely gone, and the chamber half full of rubbish. The first two rooms are clear, and can be entered without difficulty.

[3] Many of the scenes on the wall were copied by Cham-pollion and Rosellini when the sculptures were more com-plete. These older copies are therefore very valuable. They are reproduced in Rosellini's *Monumenti Civili* and Champollion's *Monuments de l'Égypte et de la Nubie*. Brugsch preserves a few of the short legends accompanying the scenes in his *Recueil de Monuments* ii. pl. lxviii. c, d, e.

considerable that it can only be accounted for by direct borrowing from the tomb of Aba at Deir el Gebrâwi. A copy, in the strict sense, it cannot be called, for many changes in detail have been made. The scenes have been re-distributed, one or two groups have been omitted, figures and objects have been given slightly different forms or positions, and some of the inscriptions have been omitted or abbreviated. Some new material has also been appended to the original scenes, largely with the object of showing the manufacture of such articles of burial furniture as were not in use in Old Kingdom days, or were not depicted at Deir el Gebrâwi. These additional scenes occupy the whole of the topmost register and the end of the second and third. This series may also have been taken from another tomb, for the operation of melting metal is introduced a second time. Besides the changes mentioned there is a great alteration in appearance due to the employment of sculpture instead of mural painting. It may be said, therefore, that a copy of the subject at Deir el Gebrâwi lay before the sculptor of this tomb, but that while he endeavoured to make use of all the figures and groups in it, he contented himself with copying the action and attitude of each, and did not hesitate to substitute familiar forms for those which were no longer known, as in the case of vases, chests, scales, &c. Where no good reason for alteration existed, the exact attitude was almost invariably retained by him.

The figure of Aba, which stands at the head of the scene, is incised like the rest, the whole ground having been first laid out in squares for the guidance of the designer. Aba carries staff and sceptre, and wears the simple tunic, the lector's scarf, a collar and pendant amulet. The descriptive text overhead is taken from the earlier tomb, with small differences of wording and spelling, the titles of Aba being replaced by that of his later namesake, who describes himself simply as " Chief Steward of the Queen."

The scenes in the FIRST REGISTER are not copied from Deir el Gebrâwi; indeed some of them could not be found in any Old Kingdom model. First are seen the metal workers, who raise their furnaces to a high temperature by the use of blowpipes.[1] Behind them are three men who sit in a circle and beat out metal (on an anvil?) with handleless hammers, which they grasp by the middle. The men above them seem to be receiving and keeping ward over the pieces of metal, which, when delivered to them, are spread out on a table (or placed in a chest?). The metal appears to be in ingots and rings; its yellow colour seems to indicate that it is gold, or perhaps electrum. Next in order are two men who carry what, to judge by shape and colour, may be a piece of matting for use as a screen. An overseer, comfortably crouched on a raised platform, superintends the work. The occupation of the two workmen behind is not easy to determine. It may be that the mass which is being mixed in the dish is the paste which was used in the manufacture of shabti figures and other small objects and afterwards glazed.[2] His companion is moulding or fitting together an elaborate coloured ornament, the chief part of which is in the form of a lily with water drops hanging from it—a type only known at a late date. A box to hold their productions, and a tool or partly finished object lie near the workmen. Next are seen the four canopic jars, inscribed for Aba, and naming the four deities who preside over their contents : they appear to be the work of the maker of shabti figures, " the chief designer, attached to the room (?) of the Queen, Pedihorsamtaui."[3] The little vase which is in the hands of the artificer

---

[1] Ros. *M. C.* lii. fig. 3.

[2] Or is it paint which is being ground on a slab ?

[3] Ros. *M. C.* xlv. 5. Neither the shabtis nor the canopic jars can have been copied from an early tomb.

behind may be of the same material. His fellow workman seems to be making a stand or coffer for the vase, the height of which he is noticing : he is at the same time measuring off lengths on a strip of wood, which he holds on his knees. His method of measurement is interesting, his unit being the forearm from the wrist to the elbow. Having already measured off this length with one arm, he is about to do the same with the other ; or else he is computing the remainder by means of the span between thumb and finger, thus using the natural divisions of length, on which primitive metrology is based. It is possible, however, that this interpretation of the action is altogether at fault. The rest of the register is occupied by leather workers, who are making the sandals with which the dead was furnished. The man on the right is pulling a strip of hide to and fro over a rounded saddle set on legs. A bearded comrade is holding out a pair of finished sandals for inspection. The inscriptions perhaps read, " leather of fox-skin," " leather of goat-skin," but the second is blundered. Two others are cutting out leather by means of broad-headed and handled knives of a peculiar shape, which cut by a rocking rather than a drawing action. One is cutting off narrow strips on a board ; the other seems to be shaping something out of a skin, which he has spread'out upon the ground. The inscription reads " cutting up a leopard-skin." [1]

In the SECOND REGISTER the stone workers and carpenters are represented, who occupy the topmost register at Deir el Gebrâwi (Plates xiii., xiv.). The second group of carpenters is omitted, as well as the greater part of the legend over the preceding group.[2] Considerable changes have been made in the shapes of the vases, but the forms have been selected to correspond as closely as possible to the obsolete types of the Old Kingdom. The chest also has been given a more modern appearance. The fragment of inscription over the vases confirms the reading already adopted for the earlier text (p. 19). The two groups of the sculptor at work on the sitting statue, and of his companion with the bird, are almost entirely destroyed. The rest of the register contains matter new to the VIth Dynasty tomb. As the contents of the first naos were not shown, another is depicted, in which the standing statue of the deceased is being set. Further on are two wheelwrights fitting together one of the wheels of a chariot.[3] The axle-tree with the floor or front of the car already attached to it lies behind them with two bent hoops of wood to be used in the framework. Another workman with his adze trims down a slender pole against a large wooden block; it is, no doubt, to be used in the bent woodwork of the frame. Two others hold similar, but thicker poles, one end of which they have inserted between two upright posts fixed in the ground, so that they can bend or straighten the poles at will. The two wheels shown in the background, as well as the action represented, indicate that the two lengths of wood are being bent round to form the rim of the wheel. By bending the two in opposite directions at the same time, in the way shown here, the strain on the upright posts is reduced to a minimum.[4]

The THIRD REGISTER contains the scenes of the second register of the wall at Deir el Gebrâwi (Plates xiii., xiv.).[5] The operation of stringing beadwork and cleaning the collars does not seem to have been fully considered, or has been carelessly rendered ; for the articles in the hands of the men, and set out on the

---

[1] Ros. M. C. lxiv. fig. 4. Champ. Mon. clxxxii.

[2] The group is complete with the inscription in Champ. Mon. clxxxi. 1, and the naos scene is in fig. 4 of the same plate.

[3] Ros. Mon. Civ. xliv. 4. Champ. Mon. cxcii. 2. The wheel had seven spokes.

[4] Ros. Mon. Civ. xliv. 4. Champ. Mon. cxcii. 1.

[5] The stand with vases in Champ. Mon. clxxxi. fig. 2.

tables behind them, are so roughly outlined as to be deprived of all meaning. The tables also on which the collars were being handled have been transformed into coffers.[1] Although the wrecked state of the wall forbids certainty, all the groups in the original seem to have been faithfully reproduced here; for the most part with the same superscriptions. The standing statue which is being chiselled by the sculptor seems to be that of a man.[2] Even the couchant lion, probably significant only at Deir el Gebrâwi, is copied in this Theban tomb.[3] The broken inscription over the second statue has apparently been replaced by the name of a contemporary craftsman, but this also is almost obliterated.[4]

Beyond the group of table-polishers were several scenes added from other sources, or at the artist's fancy. The first of these is still connected with the preceding scene, for it shows a carpenter fashioning the leg of a table with the adze on a wooden block.[5] The inscription over it, " A carpenter working with the adze," is the repetition of one preceding it; further on, over a lost scene, the later determinative is added to the verb. Apparently, therefore, the intention was to copy the original legend, without change.

The scenes of the FOURTH REGISTER, representing shipwrights and workers in precious materials, are taken from the third and fourth registers of the wall at Deir el Gebrâwi (Plates xvi., xiii., xiv.). The two last groups of the fourth register there are placed first here, but in reverse order. On these there evidently

followed the whole of the third register of the original; but the first three groups after the weighing scene are entirely destroyed. The attitudes of the men who carry the great baulk of timber have been slightly altered, and the second labourer has been given a specially elaborate toilette.[6] The form of the balance had evidently somewhat altered in the long lapse of time, and the sculptor has represented the appliance as he knew it. The post is here surmounted by a human head and the substances are weighed in scales, instead of in baskets attached to hooks. The pointer is here destroyed. The weight shown in the scales is in the form of an ibex.[7] In the superscription over the melters of metal at the end of the row,[8] a sign which is not clear in the original at Deir el Gebrâwi has been read, rightly or wrongly, by the Theban copyist as ⸱; further on a ⸱ has been left out by him.

The FIFTH REGISTER is occupied by scribes and shipbuilders, comprising probably the whole of the fifth and what remained of the fourth registers of the original (Plates xv., xvi.). The greater part of it is now destroyed. The inscriptions over the scribes contain several errors, which seem to indicate that the paintings at Deir el Gebrâwi had even at that time sustained many of the present injuries. The first legend is probably a mistaken copy of ⸱, but it is not apparent why a meaningless sign has been prefixed to the second superscription. In the third instance ⸱ has been mistaken for ⸱. The inscription over the last figure in the row[9] (a man who

---

[1] Ros. *Mon. Civ.* li. figs. 1, 2.

[2] Ros. *M. C.* xlvi. 9. Champ. *Mon.* clxxx. 1. The statue is backed against a pilaster. Rosellini makes it represent a woman, Champollion a man.

[3] Ros. *M. C.* xlvii. 1. Champ. *Mon.* clxxx. 3.

[4] Ros. *M. C.* xlvi. 8, Champ. *Mon.* clxxx. 2, give the group complete; the scribe standing behind (as in Pl. xiv.) in Champ. *Mon.* clxxxiii. 2; after this must have come the ⸱ group of Champ. *Mon.* clxxxiii. 1.

[5] Champ. *Mon.* clxxx. 4.

[6] The finer details of the tunic have had to be omitted in the Plate. The boat-building is given in Ros. *Mon. Civ.* xliv. 2, Champ. *Mon.* clxxxiii. 3; the carrying of the timber in Ros. *Mon. Civ.* xlvii. 5.

[7] Nearly complete in Ros. *Mon. Civ.* li. 3.

[8] As in Pl. xiv.

[9] Cf. Pl. xvi. top right-hand corner.

is working at the end of the boat) has been abbreviated and altered, but the new form has for us no more meaning than the old, and may merely be the result of a careless reading of the faded signs. There is abundant reason to believe that the artist did not hesitate to set down what was incomprehensible to him.

Hunting Scene (Plate xxv.). On the east wall of the third chamber there is a small scene which also seems to have had its origin in the tomb at Deir el Gebrâwi. It is a hunting scene, and its prototype will be found in the top register on Plate xi. The Theban artist has used considerable freedom in his reproduction of the picture, and it has besides suffered many injuries; but there remains sufficient similarity to make the comparison profitable, having in view the sadly defaced condition of the original. The omissions from the picture suggest anew that at the time of the XXVIth Dynasty the defacement had already progressed so far that it was impossible to obtain a complete copy, and that vacant spaces were left to be filled at the caprice of the designer. No inscriptions have been inserted by him. The animals here represented are two (?) maned lions, each (?) of which is striking down a gazelle, a leopard, two hunting dogs, a pair of oryxes struck by the arrows of the hunter, a hedgehog of unnatural proportions and a gazelle. Two hunters, armed with bows and arrows, follow the chase. The first is kneeling on one knee, the better to discharge his shaft; the other is not, as in the original, holding a hound in leash, but carries a bow and quiver, and holds spare arrows ready in his hand.

The simple fact of this copy having been made at this period throws an interesting light on the ideas of the men of the time regarding the work of their distant ancestors, and on their ability or willingness to reproduce the art of the Old Kingdom. In many respects it affords a striking testimony to the continuity and conservatism of the Egyptian civilization, that such a representation, involving, as it does, close connections with the domestic economy, the arts and crafts, and the religious customs of the people, should, with but little change or addition, be considered a suitable depiction of a corresponding scene after the lapse of 2000 years.[1]

The accompanying reproduction, which has been made with a view to the comparison of the copy with the original in all detail, will probably afford opportunity for many an interesting study alike of the changes and of the lack of change which the long history of the Egyptian nation exhibits. Perhaps it may also aid in the detection of similar instances in which the XXVIth Dynasty borrowed its exemplars from the Ancient Kingdom.

---

[1] But here it behoves us to be cautious. The XXVIth Dynasty was a period of archaistic revival; and in any case the unsystematic Egyptian could not be expected to bring his designs thoroughly "up to date" in reproducing them. It has been pointed out incidentally in *Beni Hasan*, part iv. p. 6, that bellows were known and regularly used by metal workers in the XVIIIth Dynasty, replacing the old method of blowing through canes. It is most improbable that the old and very unsatisfactory mode was ever again revived. The furnace blowers with their canes in the tomb of Aba at Thebes must be a strong instance of archaistic anachronism.—Ed.

INDEX.

(Proper Names occurring in the Tombs are printed in Capitals.)

E

PRINTED BY GILBERT AND RIVINGTON, LTD., ST. JOHN'S HOUSE, CLERKENWELL, E.C.

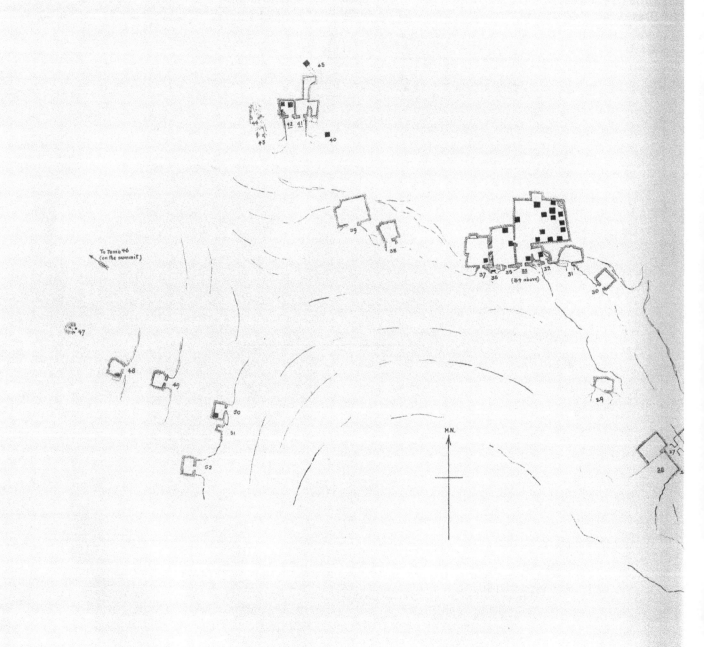

PLATE I.

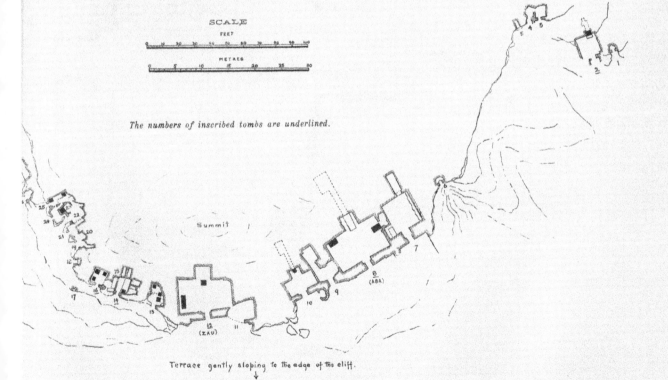

SCALE

FEET

METRES

The numbers of inscribed tombs are underlined.

Summit

Terrace gently sloping to the edge of the cliff.

PLATE II.

DEIR EL GEBRÂWI I.

TOMB OF ABA.

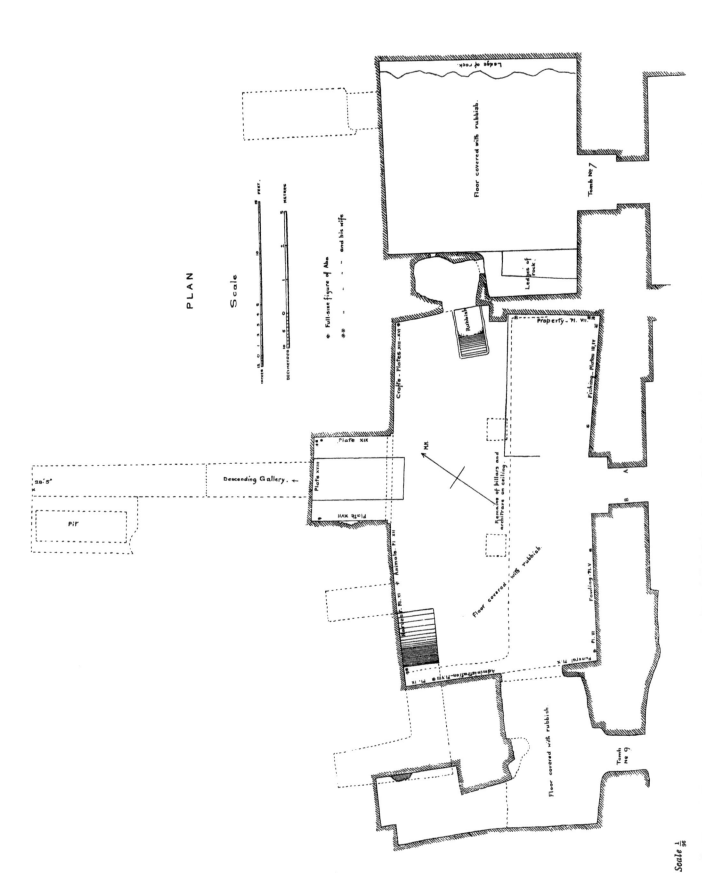

PLAN

Scale

✳ Full-size figure of Aba
✳✳ „ „ „ „ and his wife

Scale 1/96

TOMB OF ABA.

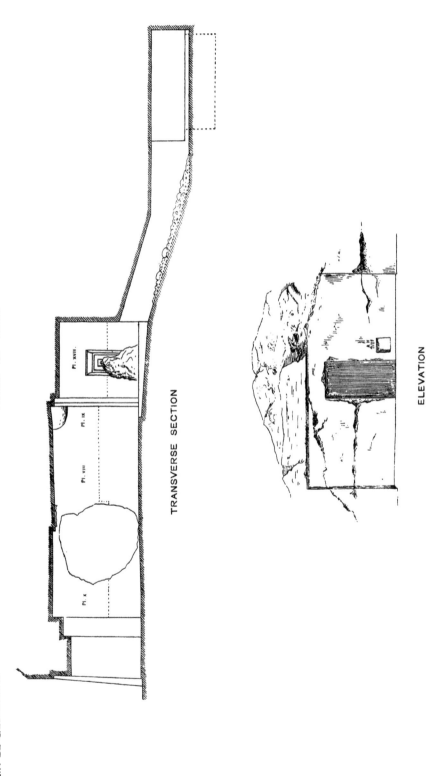

TRANSVERSE SECTION

ELEVATION

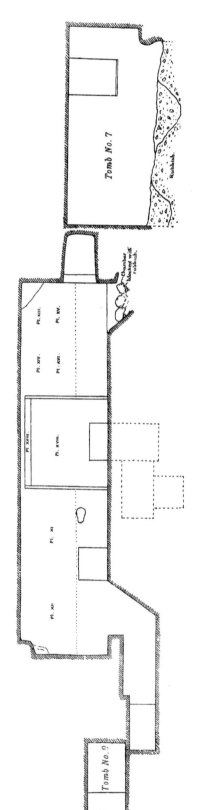

LONGITUDINAL SECTION

Scale $\frac{1}{96}$

Plate IV.

boulder

a

b

Plate III.

SOUTH WALL, WEST

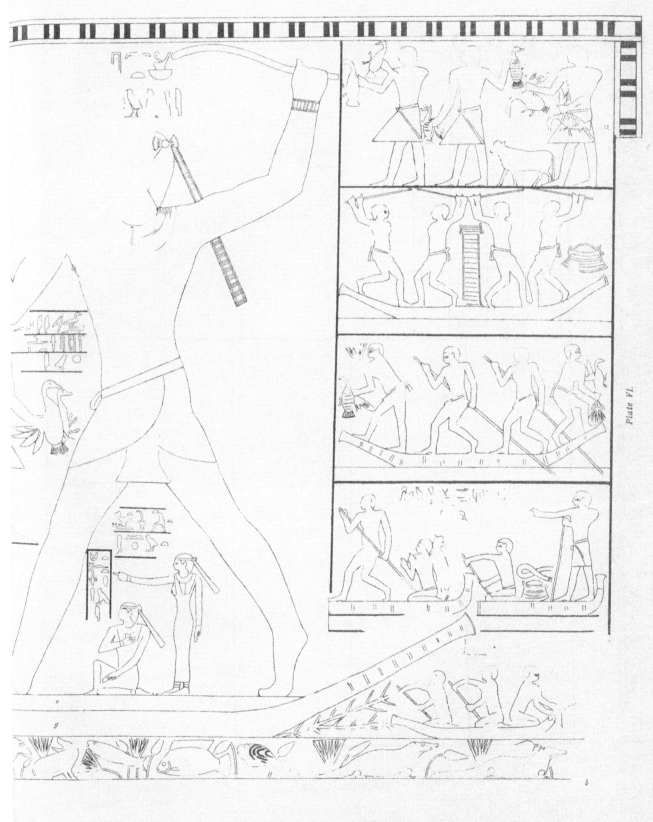

Plate VI.

SIDE—LEFT HALF.

PLATE VI.

DEIR EL GEBRÂWI I.

TOMB OF ABA.

Plate V.

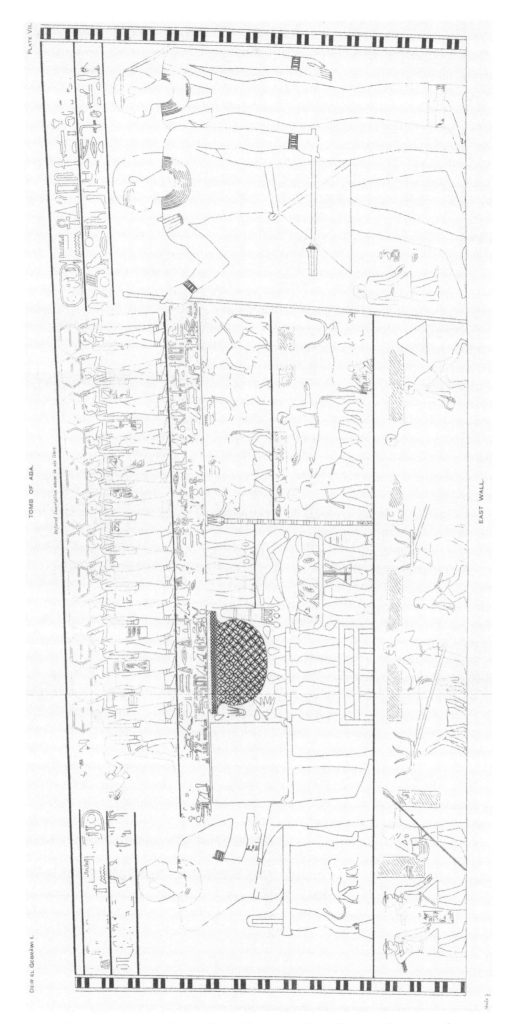

The material originally positioned here is too large for reproduction in this reissue. A PDF can be downloaded from the web address given on page iv of this book, by clicking on 'Resources Available'.

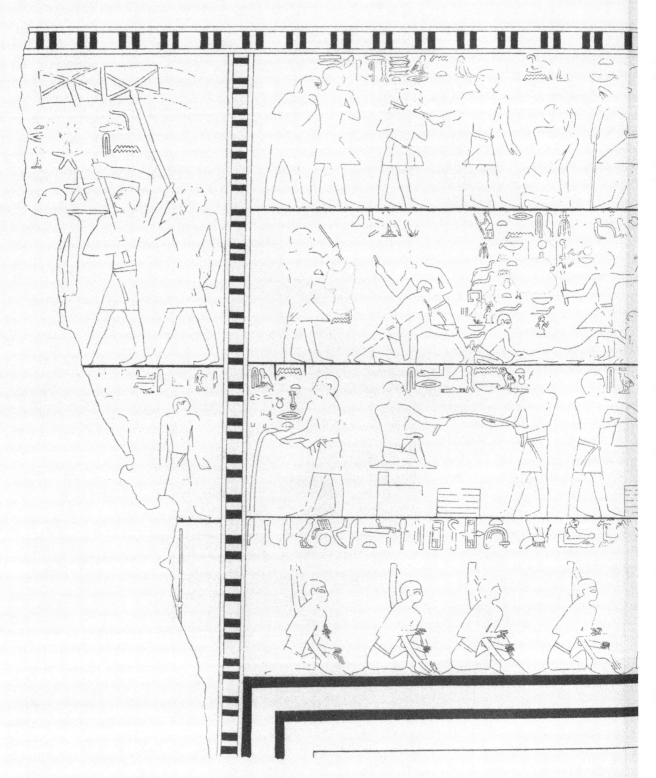

Scale ⅙th

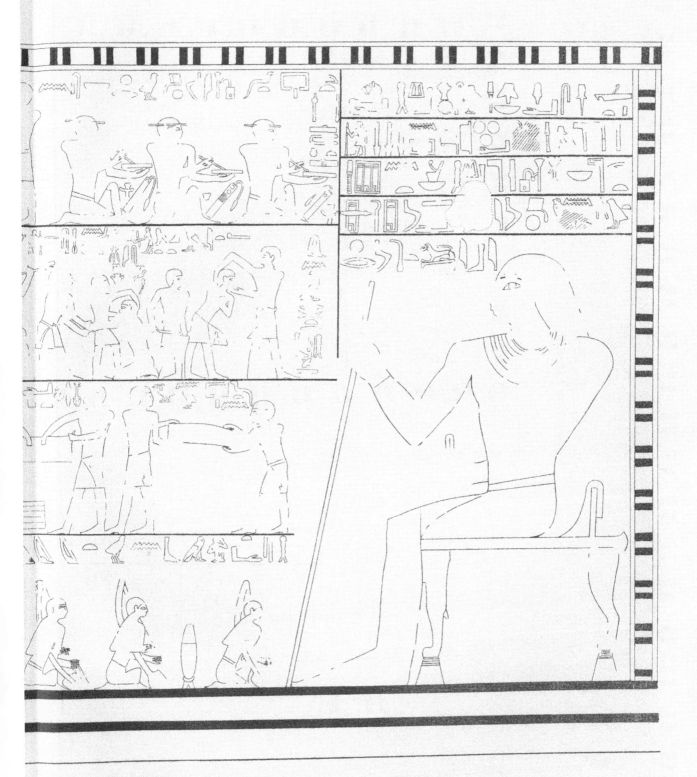

PLATE IX.

TOMB OF ABA.

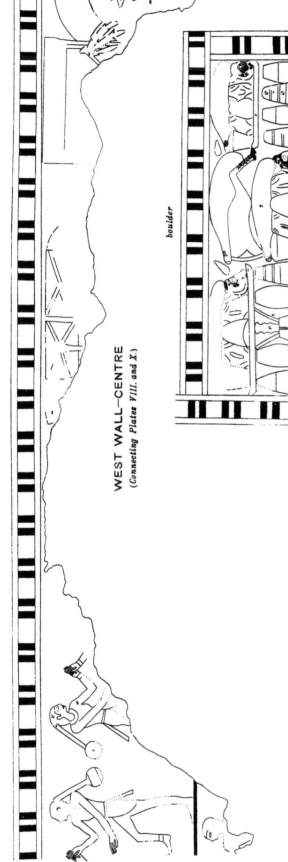

WEST WALL—CENTRE

(Connecting Plates VIII. and X.)

boulder

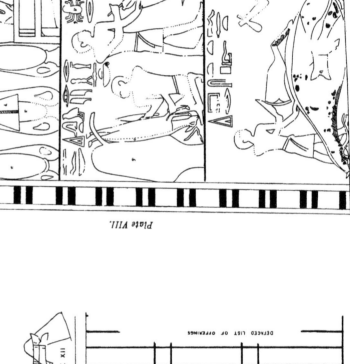

Plate VIII.

WEST WALL—N. END.

DEFACED LIST OF OFFERINGS

PLATE XII

NORTH WALL—W, END.

Scale $\frac{1}{6}$

WEST WALL—S. PORTION.

Plate XII.

a

b

NORTH WALL,

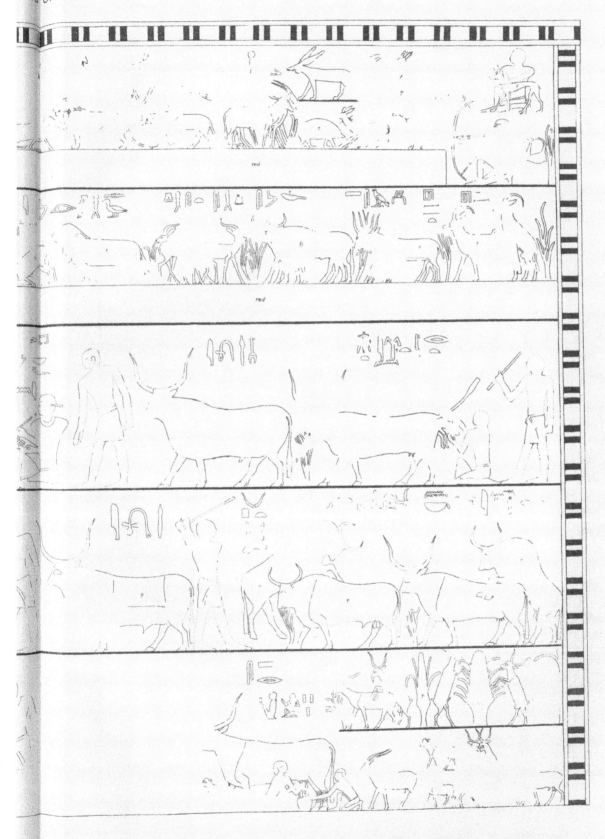

WEST SIDE—RIGHT HALF.

The upper part of th

Boulder

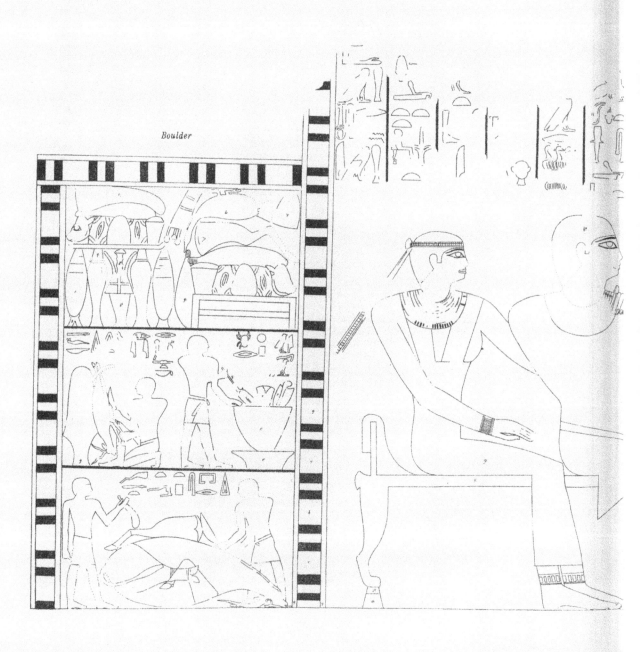

e scene is obliterated.

Plate XI.

ST SIDE—LEFT HALF.

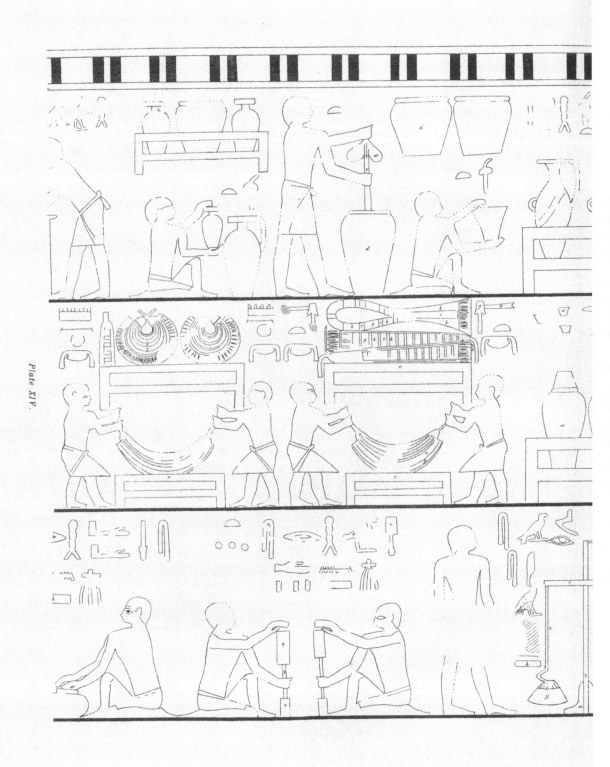

Plate XIV.

NORTH WALL, EAST SIDE. U

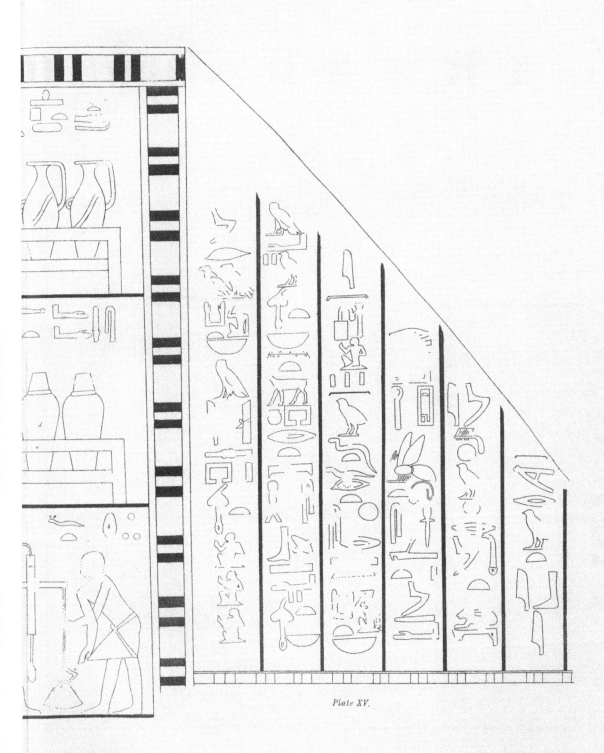

Plate XV.

PPER REGISTERS—RIGHT HALF

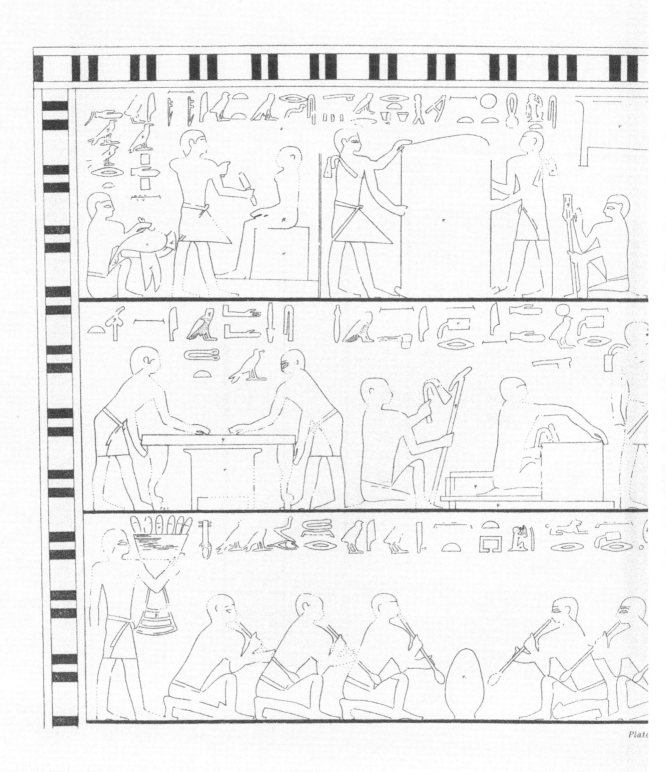

Plate

Scale ¼

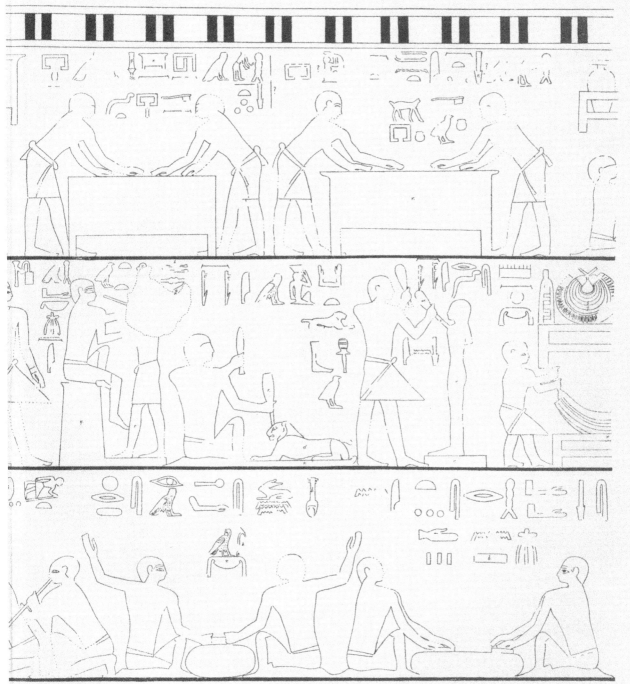

Plate XIII.

XVI.

UPPER REGISTERS—COMPLETION.

Plate XIII.

Plate XVI.

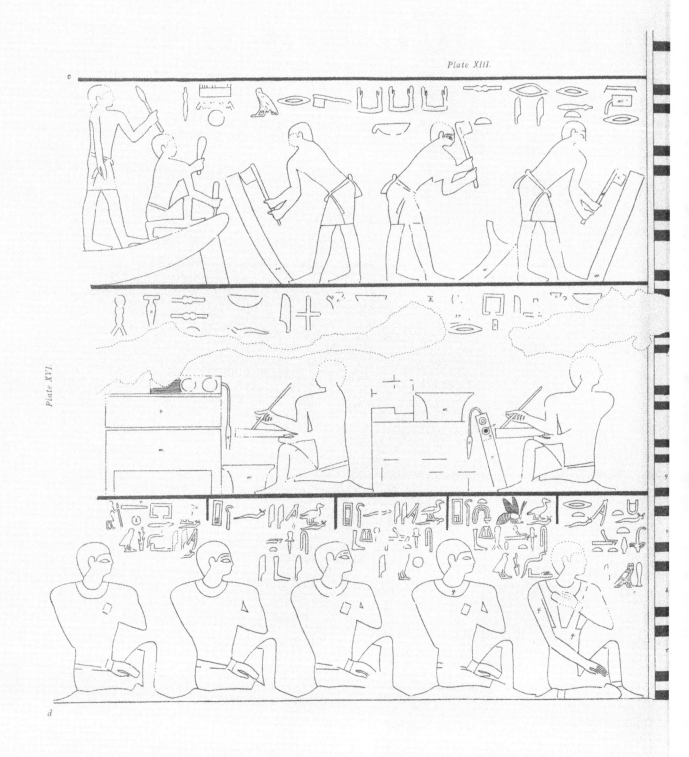

Scale ⅛

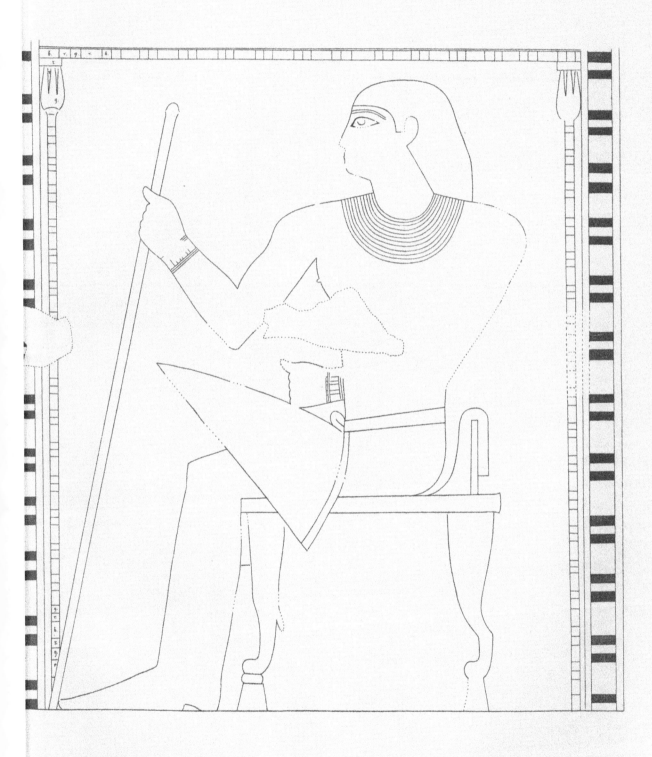

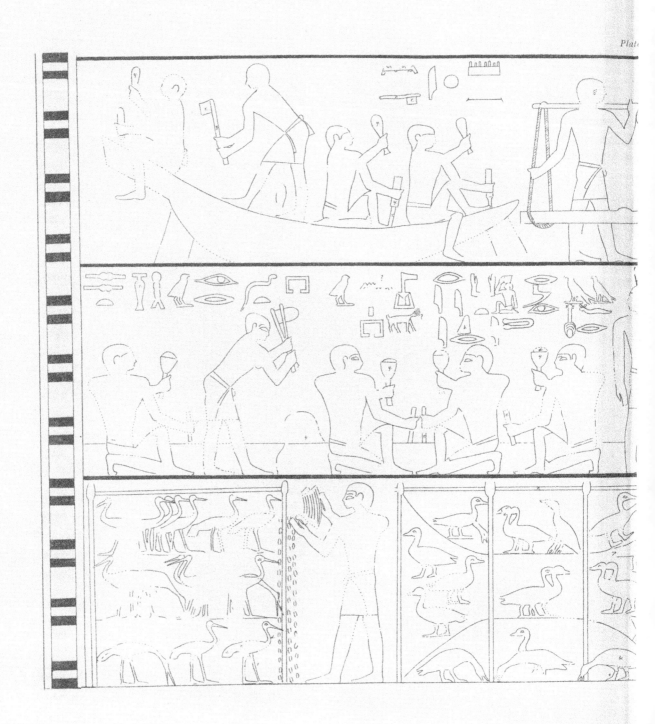

PLATE XVI.

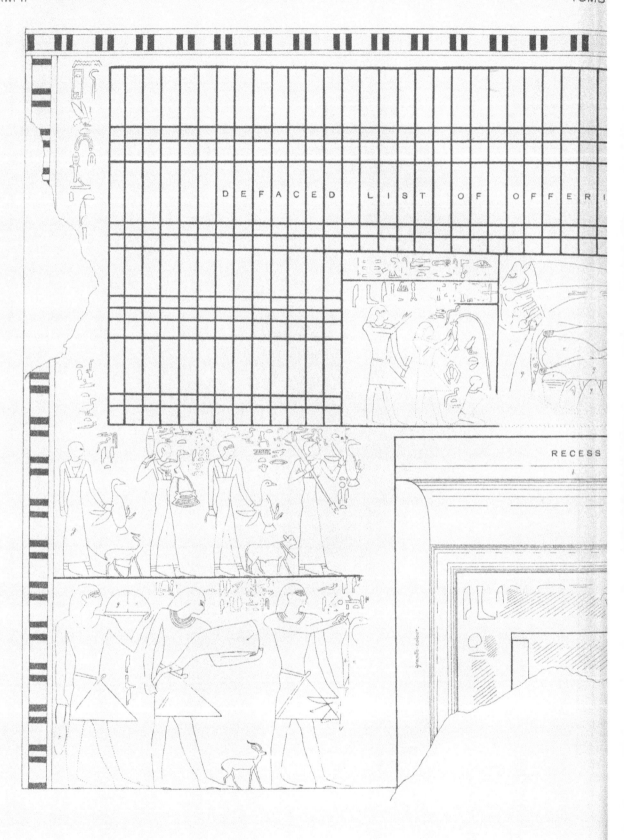

DEFACED   LIST   OF   OFFERI

RECESS

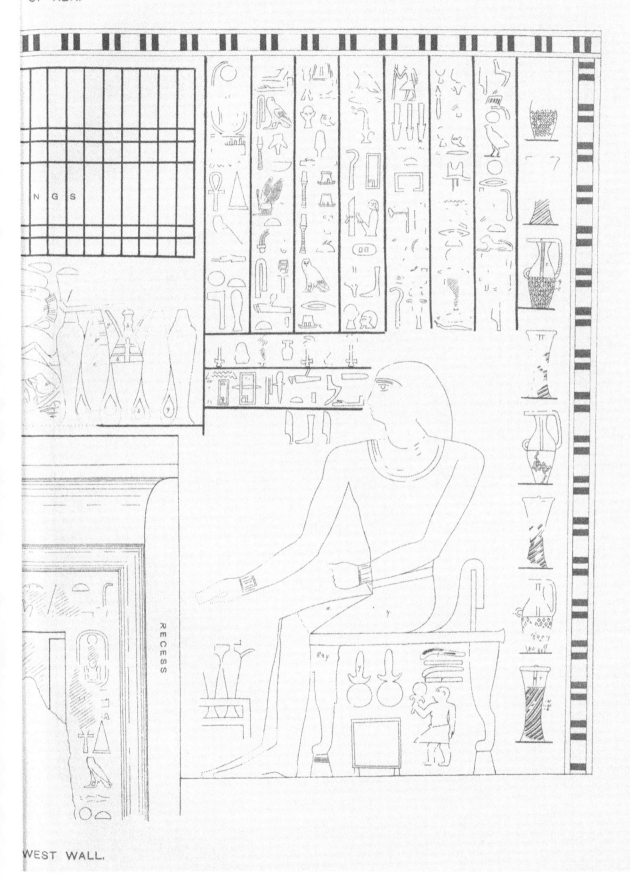

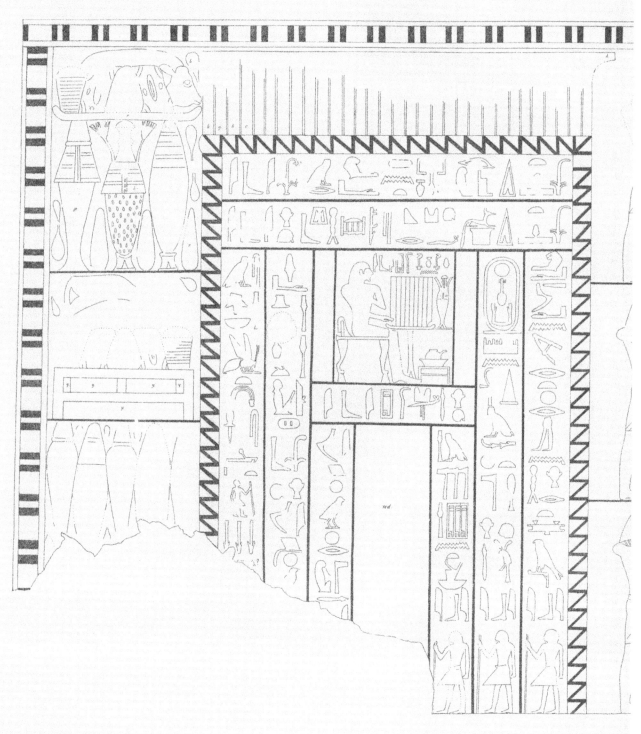

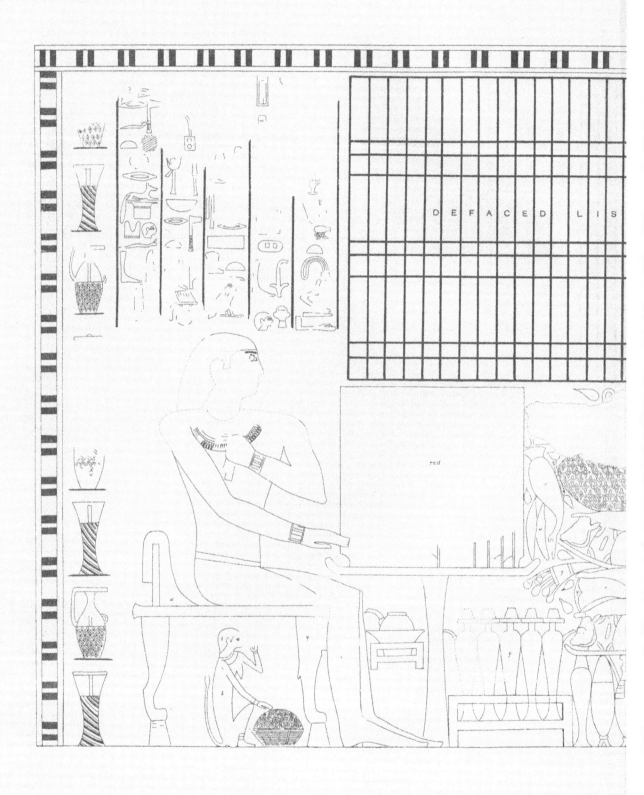

DEFACED LIS

red

Scale ⅛

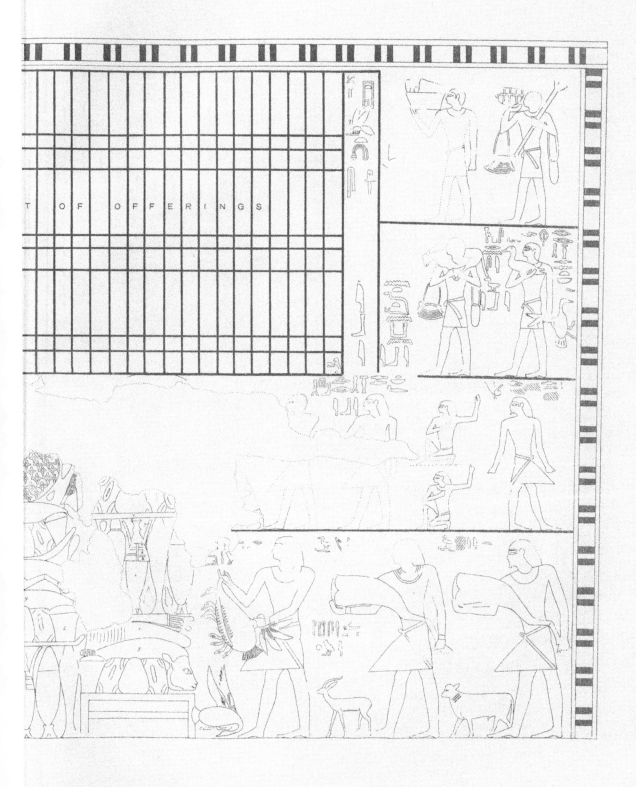

T OF OFFERINGS

PLATE XX.

PREPARING FISH.

(*See Plate IV.*).

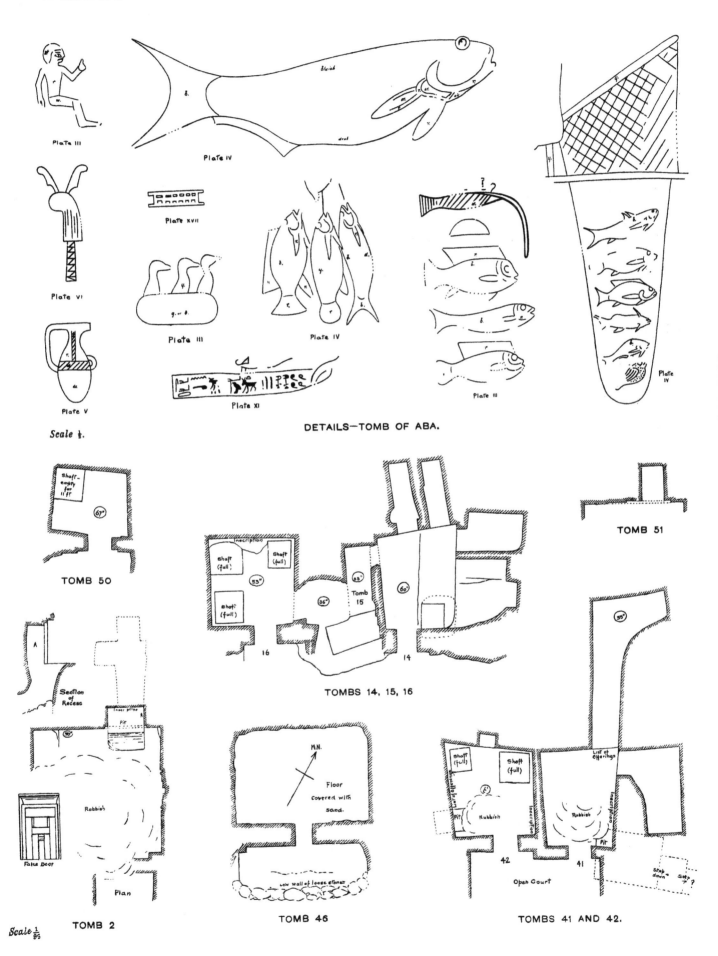

Plate III

Plate IV

Plate XVII

Plate VI

Plate III

Plate IV

Plate III

Plate IV

Plate V

Plate XI

Scale ⅛.

DETAILS—TOMB OF ABA.

TOMB 50

TOMB 51

TOMBS 14, 15, 16

TOMB 2

TOMB 46

TOMBS 41 AND 42.

Scale 1/85

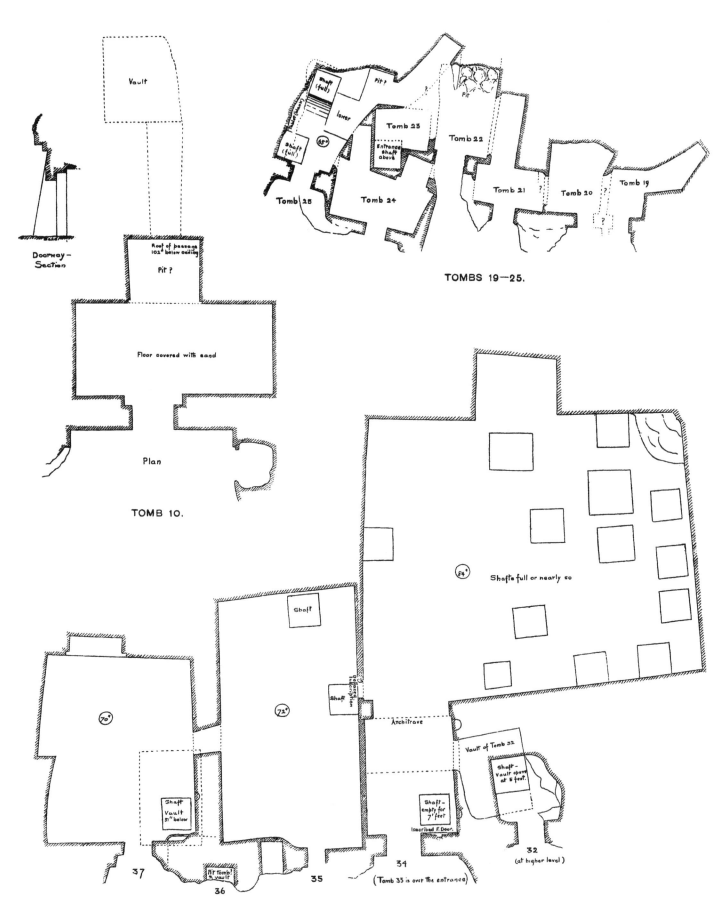

TOMBS 19—25.

Doorway—Section

TOMB 10.

TOMBS 32—37.

Scale 1/96

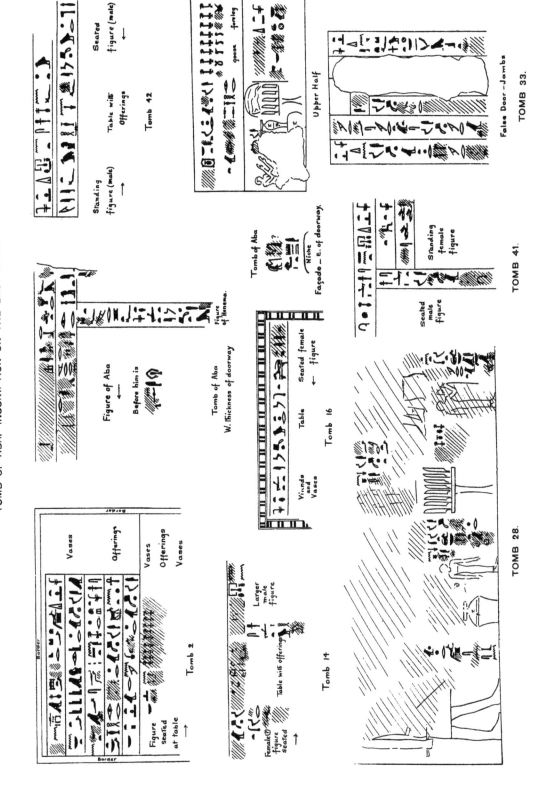

DEIR EL GEBRÂWI.

PLATE XXIII.

FRAGMENTARY INSCRIPTIONS.

TOMB OF ABA. INSCRIPTION ON THE EAST WALL

Figure of Aba

Before him is

Tomb of Aba
W. thickness of doorway.

Figure of Henema.

Tomb 2

Border

Border

Vases

Offerings

Vases
Offerings
Vases

Figure seated at table

Tomb 14

Larger male figure

Table with offerings

Female(?) figure seated

Tomb 16

Viands and Vases

Table

Seated female figure

Tomb of Aba
Niche
Façade — E. of doorway.

Tomb 42

Standing figure (male)

Table with Offerings

Seated figure (male)

Upper Half

goose forcing

Standing female figure

Seated male figure

TOMB 41.

TOMB 33.

False Door-Jambs

TOMB 28.

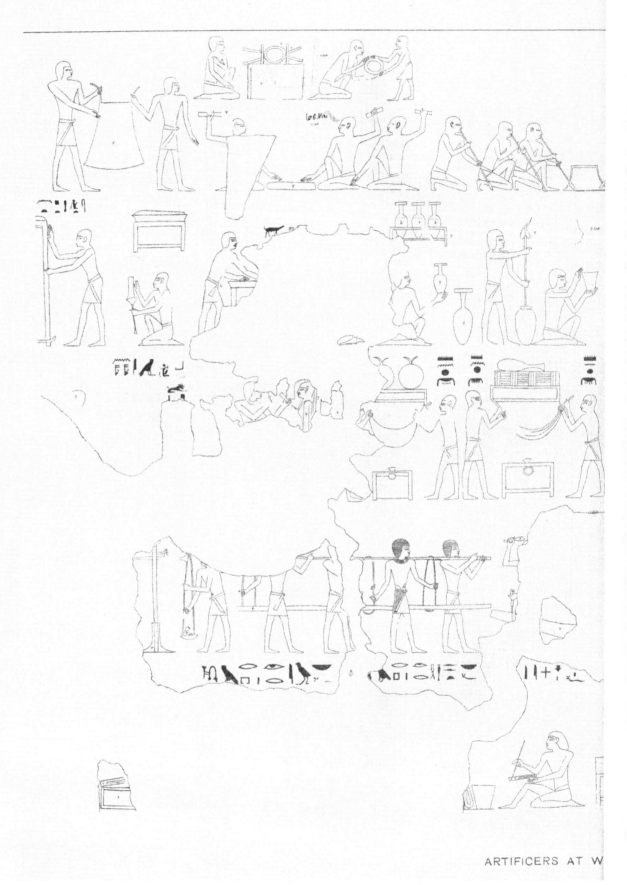

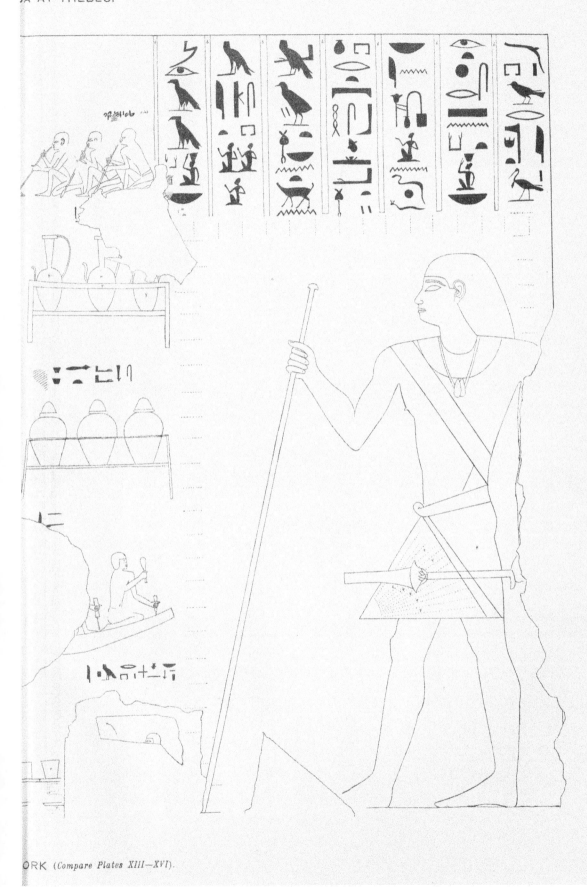

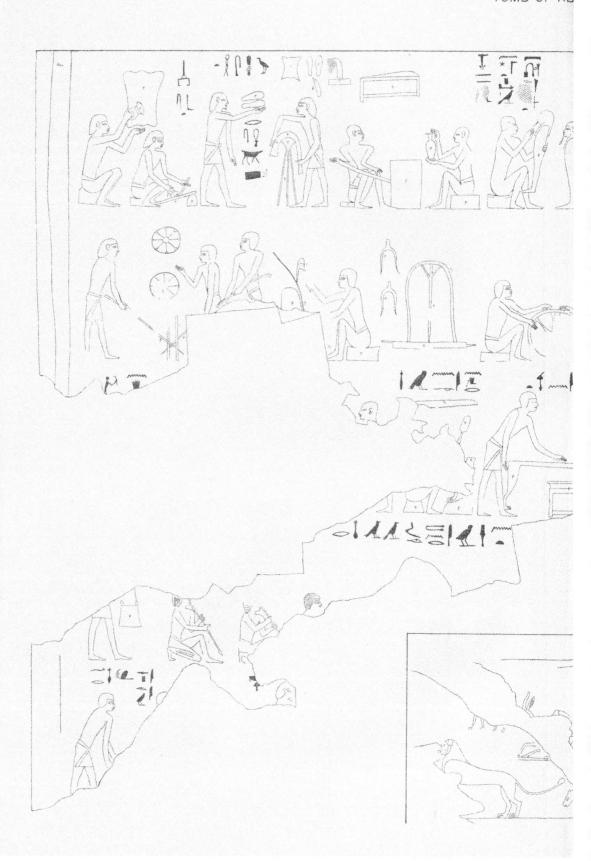

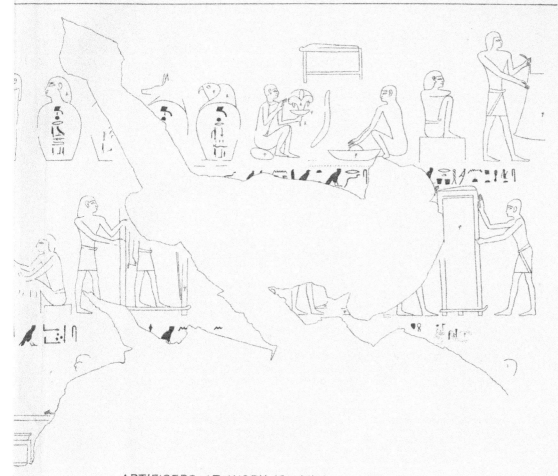

ARTIFICERS AT WORK (*Completion*).

DESERT SCENE (*Compare Plate XI*).

For EU product safety concerns, contact us at Calle de José Abascal, 56–1°,
28003 Madrid, Spain or eugpsr@cambridge.org.

www.ingramcontent.com/pod-product-compliance
Ingram Content Group UK Ltd.
Pitfield, Milton Keynes, MK11 3LW, UK
UKHW051030150625
459647UK00023B/2872